VMware Horizon View Essentials

Successfully design, install, and configure an end-to-end VDI infrastructure with VMware Horizon View

Peter von Oven

BIRMINGHAM - MUMBAI

VMware Horizon View Essentials

First published: October 2014

Production reference: 1201014

Published by Packt Publishing Ltd.
Livery Place
35 Livery Street
Birmingham B3 2PB, UK.

ISBN 978-1-78439-936-8

www.packtpub.com

Credits

Author
Peter von Oven

Reviewers
Biswapati Bhattacharjee
Abhilash HB
J. Powell

Commissioning Editor
Ashwin Nair

Acquisition Editor
Owen Roberts

Content Development Editor
Adrian Raposo

Technical Editors
Mrunal M. Chavan
Gaurav Thingalaya

Copy Editors
Relin Hedly
Stuti Srivastava

Project Coordinator
Kinjal Bari

Proofreaders
Simran Bhogal
Stephen Copestake
Elinor Perry-Smith

Indexers
Hemangini Bari
Mariammal Chettiyar
Tejal Soni

Graphics
Ronak Dhruv

Production Coordinator
Manu Joseph

Cover Work
Manu Joseph

About the Author

Peter von Oven is an experienced technical consultant and has spent the last 20 years of his IT career working with customers and partners, designing technology solutions aimed at delivering true business value. Throughout his career, he has been involved with numerous large-scale enterprise projects and deployments, presented at key IT events, and worked in senior presales roles for some of the giants of IT. Over the last 8 years, he has focused his skills and experience on the desktop virtualization market. Today, he not only leads the End User Computing Systems Engineering team at VMware UK&I—delivering the next generation of end user computing and mobile cloud solutions—but is also the SE manager of the partner and general business SE team.

Peter got his first taste of writing when assisting with some of the chapters in *Building End-User Computing Solutions with VMware View*, *Mike Laverick and Barry Coombs, Mike Laverick Ltd*. Later, he wrote *VMware Horizon Mirage Essentials* and co-authored *VMware Horizon Workspace Essentials*; both of these books were published by Packt Publishing. He is currently co-authoring *Mastering VMware Horizon, Packt Publishing*, which will be published in late 2014.

I would like to dedicate this book to the memory of my late grandmother, who passed away at the beginning of 2014, sadly. She was an inspiration to me and could always be relied upon for her support, advice, and words of wisdom. She will be truly missed.

There are also a couple of people I want to thank for the continued and ongoing support they have given me during the writing of this book. Firstly, and most importantly, I would like to thank my wife and our two young daughters for their continued support while I spent evenings and weekends writing—I couldn't have done this without your support. Secondly, thanks to the Packt Publishing team for giving me the opportunity to write this book and for their support, which has been outstanding yet again.

About the Reviewers

Biswapati Bhattacharjee is a seasoned professional in the field of information technology. So far, he has played many roles in various domains in his professional life, ranging from quality engineering, performance benchmarking, presales technical, and project management to customer interaction, ISV partner management, and technical consultancy. He has worked on many projects with different teams spread across the globe.

Biswapati has extensive experience in VMware VDI. He was part of the QA team when VMware acquired Propero's desktop solution product and released VDM 2.0. In addition to VDI, he worked with VMware ISV partners in the areas of server, BCDR, and cloud solutions for the performance and functional validation of ISV products.

He is also a speaker at VMworld, where he has discussed VMware Virtual SAN™ and ISV applications' performance characterization in the areas of VMware Horizon View and VMware VDI solutions. He has many published papers and deployment guides on ISV applications in VMware-virtualized platforms.

He received his Bachelors of Engineering degree from Regional Engineering College (now National Institute of Technology), India. He can be found on LinkedIn at www.linkedin.com/in/biswapatibhattacharjee/. This is his first book review.

I would like to thank my wife, Chandrima, for her continuous encouragement and support and our lovely daughter, Bidushi, who never fails to inspire me.

I also want to thank my parents—Gauri (my mom) and Nishithendu (my dad)—for always believing in me and my brothers—Basudeb and Vivekananda—for their guidance.

I take this opportunity to express my gratitude to all the people who have been instrumental in the successful completion of this book review. This critical work would not have been possible without my extended family—my sisters-in-law, Pompa and Nivedita; my niece, Satakshi; my nephew, Vishok; my brother in-law, Chitrarath; and my parents-in-law, Ratna and Chinmoy.

Abhilash HB is a passionate cloud services engineer who loves virtualization and cloud computing. He is an avid blogger at `http://vpirate.in`. VMware has recognized him as a VMware vExpert under the Evangelist Path for his contribution to the virtualization and cloud computing communities through knowledge sharing and content creation. He is also recognized as a PernixPro™ by PernixData. He is an expert contributor at `https://www.1cloudroad.com`.

He holds numerous technical certifications from EMC, VMware, Cisco, Microsoft, and Rackspace. He is an active member of the VMTN community.

You can follow him on Twitter at `@abhilashhb` or on LinkedIn at `in.linkedin.com/in/abhilashhb/`.

J. Powell is an active proponent of VMware's virtualization technologies for small businesses and nonprofit organizations with a focus on Horizon View and vCenter. He is a senior system engineer at Nine Virtual Technologies (`www.ninevirtualtech.com`).

He has over a decade of IT experience in enterprise infrastructure design, implementation, and administration. He holds certifications from VMware and is active on their community forums.

In addition to his IT experience, he has owned and operated a fine-dining restaurant in North Carolina, the Fifty Fifty Lounge and Grill. He currently resides in Indianapolis, Indiana, with his beautiful wife, Dena, and their daughter, Parker.

www.PacktPub.com

Support files, eBooks, discount offers, and more

You might want to visit www.PacktPub.com for support files and downloads related to your book.

Did you know that Packt offers eBook versions of every book published, with PDF and ePub files available? You can upgrade to the eBook version at www.PacktPub.com and as a print book customer, you are entitled to a discount on the eBook copy. Get in touch with us at service@packtpub.com for more details.

At www.PacktPub.com, you can also read a collection of free technical articles, sign up for a range of free newsletters and receive exclusive discounts and offers on Packt books and eBooks.

http://PacktLib.PacktPub.com

Do you need instant solutions to your IT questions? PacktLib is Packt's online digital book library. Here, you can access, read and search across Packt's entire library of books.

Why subscribe?

- Fully searchable across every book published by Packt
- Copy and paste, print and bookmark content
- On demand and accessible via web browser

Free access for Packt account holders

If you have an account with Packt at www.PacktPub.com, you can use this to access PacktLib today and view nine entirely free books. Simply use your login credentials for immediate access.

Instant updates on new Packt books

Get notified! Find out when new books are published by following @PacktEnterprise on Twitter, or the *Packt Enterprise* Facebook page.

Table of Contents

Preface

It's a tricky balancing act to manage a physical desktop estate and the challenges that it brings in delivering an improved and more flexible level of service to your end users while lowering management costs. It's a near-impossible task that IT administrators face today. This is where the latest VMware technology comes into play and helps you solve these challenges.

VMware Horizon View is a platform that delivers centralized, virtual desktop machines hosted on a server running a hypervisor and located in a data center. The end user then remotely connects to their virtual desktop machine from their end point device, such as a Windows laptop, Apple Mac, or tablet device. This technology, first introduced by VMware in 2002, is what is now known as Virtual Desktop Infrastructure, or VDI.

VDI provides users with the freedom to work in a way that suits them, freeing them from the restrictions of not having to be in the office but also allowing them the choice of the device they use. This makes them more productive, and ultimately, your business more agile.

From an IT administrator's perspective, VDI allows you to centrally manage your desktop environment, from being able to manage desktop images to the ease of adding and removing user entitlements—all controlled from a single management console.

Horizon View 6.0 is VMware's latest virtual desktop solution designed to centralize and virtualize your desktop environment using the market-leading virtualization features and technology within VMware's Software-Defined Data Center (SDDC) portfolio. Horizon View 6.0 builds upon this technology platform to deliver a rich user experience, enabling BYOD, flexible working, and enhanced security, to name but a few.

Delivering an end user experience requires a different approach from other infrastructure-based initiatives. Getting this right is the key for a project to have a successful outcome, and this book will show you how.

What this book covers

Chapter 1, Introducing VDI and VMware Horizon 6.0, introduces what VDI is and how it compares with other VDI-type technologies. We will then cover the VMware VDI story and history in brief, followed by an overview of the latest solution.

Chapter 2, Horizon View 6.0 Architectural and Feature Overview, introduces you to the different components that make up the Horizon View solution. Each section will start with an overview of a specific feature or component, describing its role in the overall solution, how it fits into the infrastructure, and in some cases, take a look under the hood at how it works.

Chapter 3, Designing and Building a Horizon View 6.0 Infrastructure, starts by talking about where to start and how to run a successful pilot. Before we embark on our VDI project, we need to understand how to approach it. We then go on to look at how we design and size an environment using a real-life example scenario.

Chapter 4, Installing Horizon View 6.0, shows you how to install the Horizon View components. Each section of the installations will be shown in detail using screenshots, detailing each of the options we select and providing reasons as to why we are selecting them. You also have the opportunity to follow the installation process, as we also build out an example lab.

Chapter 5, A Guided Tour of the Horizon View Administrator Console, takes a quick guided tour of the View Administrator console. The Horizon View Administrator is a web-based management console that is used to manage your View environment, allowing you to configure infrastructure components, desktop pools, and user entitlements.

Chapter 6, Building and Optimizing Virtual Desktop Machine OS Images, looks at how to build an operating system image for use as a virtual desktop machine. We will cover the step-by-step process of building the virtual machine, optimizing it for VDI, and then preparing it for delivery to the end user. Using examples, we will build a Windows 7 virtual desktop using linked clones, a Windows 8 full-clone desktop, and a Windows 7 full-clone desktop with access to a hardware-enabled GPU.

Chapter 7, Configuring Horizon View to Deliver Virtual Desktops, follows on from the previous chapter and we will now configure and prepare Horizon View to deliver the virtual desktop machines we built in that chapter. Using the example lab, we will configure three desktop pools for our three virtual desktop machines, one for Windows 7 (a floating assignment with linked clones), one for Windows 8 (a dedicated, full clone), and finally, a manual pool with a dedicated assignment and using an NVIDIA GPU.

Chapter 8, Horizon View Clients, looks at the different options available to end users in order to allow them to connect to their virtual desktop machines, some of the advantages and disadvantages of the different options, and why it matters which one you choose. We will talk about software clients, hardware clients, thin clients, and accessing your desktop from a browser.

Chapter 9, Fine-tuning the End User Experience, covers how we can fine-tune the end user experience. With users now using virtual desktop machines, we need to make sure that the end user experience is running at its optimum level. In this chapter, we will look at how we can tune this experience, firstly with the Active Directory Group Policy templates that control the behavior of the virtual desktop machine, and then with some of the other tools that are available.

Appendix, References, contains useful links related to the official VMware documentation and tools covered in this book.

What you need for this book

To get the most out of this book, you should have some experience working as a desktop administrator with skills and knowledge in building and designing Microsoft-Windows-based environments. You should also be familiar with the VMware vSphere platform (ESXi and vCenter Server) and be comfortable with building and configuring virtual machines as well as configuring storage and networking.

Throughout the book, you have the opportunity to follow step-by-step practical guides in order to deploy Horizon View in an example lab environment. If you want to work through the practical examples, you will need the following software:

- VMware Horizon View 6.0
- vSphere 5.5 Update 1

You can download a trial copy of Horizon View 6.0 from `https://my.vmware.com/web/vmware/evalcenter?p=horizon`.

You will also need the following software to build virtual machines and deploy applications:

- Microsoft Windows Server 2008 R2 64 bit
- Microsoft Windows 7 Professional 32 bit or 64 bit
- Microsoft Windows 8.1
- Microsoft SQL Express
- Adobe Reader

Who this book is for

If you are a desktop administrator or part of an end user computing project team looking into how to get up to speed with the latest VMware Horizon View solution quickly, then this book is perfect for you and your ideal companion to deploy a solution in order to centrally manage and virtualize your desktop estate using Horizon View 6.0. You will need to have some experience in desktop management using the Microsoft Windows desktop operating systems and general Windows applications; you should also be familiar with the Active Directory, SQL, and VMware vSphere infrastructure (ESXi and vCenter Server) technology.

Conventions

In this book, you will find a number of styles of text that distinguish between different kinds of information. Here are some examples of these styles, and an explanation of their meaning.

Code words in text, database table names, folder names, filenames, file extensions, pathnames, dummy URLs, user input, and Twitter handles are shown as follows: "After installing the certificate, you will need to restart the `View Connection Server` service in order for it to pick up the certificate."

Any command-line input or output is written as follows:

```
Montereyenable.exe - enable
```

New terms and **important words** are shown in bold. Words that you see on the screen, in menus or dialog boxes for example, appear in the text like this: "Click on **OK** when you have completed the configuration."

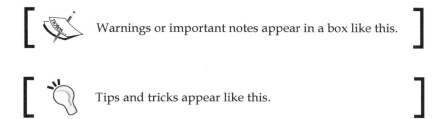

Warnings or important notes appear in a box like this.

Tips and tricks appear like this.

Reader feedback

Feedback from our readers is always welcome. Let us know what you think about this book—what you liked or may have disliked. Reader feedback is important for us to develop titles that you really get the most out of.

To send us general feedback, simply send an e-mail to feedback@packtpub.com, and mention the book title via the subject of your message.

If there is a topic that you have expertise in and you are interested in either writing or contributing to a book, see our author guide on www.packtpub.com/authors.

Customer support

Now that you are the proud owner of a Packt book, we have a number of things to help you to get the most from your purchase.

Errata

Although we have taken every care to ensure the accuracy of our content, mistakes do happen. If you find a mistake in one of our books—maybe a mistake in the text or the code—we would be grateful if you would report this to us. By doing so, you can save other readers from frustration and help us improve subsequent versions of this book. If you find any errata, please report them by visiting http://www.packtpub.com/submit-errata, selecting your book, clicking on the **errata submission form** link, and entering the details of your errata. Once your errata are verified, your submission will be accepted and the errata will be uploaded on our website, or added to any list of existing errata, under the Errata section of that title. Any existing errata can be viewed by selecting your title from http://www.packtpub.com/support.

Piracy

Piracy of copyright material on the Internet is an ongoing problem across all media. At Packt, we take the protection of our copyright and licenses very seriously. If you come across any illegal copies of our works, in any form, on the Internet, please provide us with the location address or website name immediately so that we can pursue a remedy.

Please contact us at copyright@packtpub.com with a link to the suspected pirated material.

We appreciate your help in protecting our authors, and our ability to bring you valuable content.

Questions

You can contact us at questions@packtpub.com if you are having a problem with any aspect of the book, and we will do our best to address it.

1
Introducing VDI and VMware Horizon 6.0

In this first chapter, we are going to take a look at what **virtual desktop infrastructure** (**VDI**) actually is, briefly explain the different technologies for delivering desktops and applications available today, and how they work. We will then focus specifically on the VMware solution, which is **Horizon View 6.0**, discuss its history and how it compares to other technologies such as server-based computing, before moving on to discuss some of the benefits of deploying VDI.

What is virtual desktop infrastructure?

As we touched on at the start of this chapter, there are different definitions for the solutions that fall under the heading of VDI, depending on the vendor you are working with. For example, in some cases, the term VDI is used when, in fact, the solution is just delivering applications.

The term VDI was actually adopted by VMware and has become the accepted definition for this technology. In the context of a VMware Horizon View VDI solution, this refers to a model whereby the desktop operating system is running as a virtual machine hosted on a hypervisor, which is VMware vSphere (ESXi and vCenter) in this case, and running on the server infrastructure located centrally somewhere in a data center.

Users then connect remotely to their virtual desktop machine over the LAN/WAN/
Internet from their chosen endpoint device and from any location. You might also
hear this model being referred to as the **hosted virtual desktop (HVD)** model.
This is shown in the following diagram:

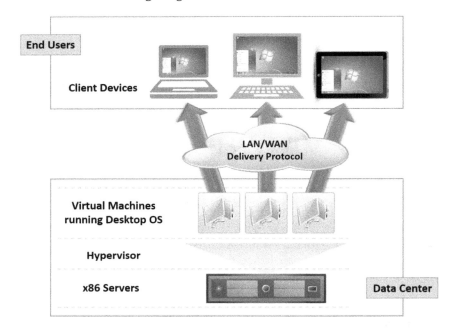

How does a user connect to their desktop?

As we just discussed, the desktop is now a virtual machine running on the server
infrastructure in the data center, so how does a user connect to and use their desktop?

From their chosen endpoint device (laptop, Mac, tablet, smart phone, and so on), the
user launches a software connection client, which connects them to the infrastructure
and authenticates their login credentials, which then delivers their desktop to the
network using an optimized delivery protocol. They can also use a hardware client
for this, and we will cover this later in the *Horizon View Clients* section in *Chapter 2,
Horizon View 6.0 Architectural and Feature Overview*. The connection can be performed
using browser-based access, which we will cover in *Chapter 8, Horizon View Clients*.

The key idea and a point to remember in a VDI solution is that, the data never leaves the data center. It's just the pixels from the virtual desktop's display that get sent over the network, and the keyboard strokes and mouse movements from the endpoint device that are redirected back to the virtual desktop machine. It's like having a very long remote control for your desktop or a very long set of cables!

Why VDI desktops are different from physical desktops

If we look at the virtual desktop machine and its basic architecture, it is subtly different when compared to a physical desktop PC and how a desktop is built and delivered. In a physical model, a user "owns" the desktop, as it's sitting on their desk. They use the same machine every day. In a VDI environment, desktops are not necessarily owned by the user and are delivered in a manner that reduces the complexity and infrastructure requirements, instead.

In a typical VDI deployment, the desktops will be part of a pool of virtual machines that are ready for a user to consume. Each desktop starts life with exactly the same image (like having a new machine) with no user personalization or customization, as the user does not own that desktop. As they log in, they are allocated a desktop from a pool that assumes their profile and becomes their desktop for that particular session. When they log off, the desktop returns to the pool ready for the next user. This means that a virtual desktop is built differently from its physical counterpart.

In terms of how the desktop is built, each virtual desktop machine is effectively assembled using its component parts, operating system, user profile, and then, applications. We often hear this being referred to as the composite desktop model, and this is shown in the following diagram:

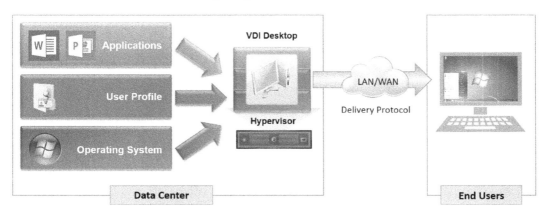

You might also find that the hardware specification of the virtual desktop machine can differ from a physical PC. As the virtual desktop machine is running on a hypervisor, you can monitor the resources it consumes more closely, allowing you to potentially lower the hardware specification. For example, some of the memory-sharing technologies found in the hypervisor can allow you to reduce the amount of memory you need for configuration.

These are just some of the high-level differences, and we will cover some of the deeper differences when we build our virtual desktop machine in *Chapter 6, Building and Optimizing Virtual Desktop Machine OS Images*, where we will look at how the operating system configuration differs from a physical PC.

At the beginning of this chapter, we mentioned that there are other technologies that are available for delivering virtual desktops and applications to deliver the end user experience. We will discuss this in the next section, starting with server-based computing.

Server-based computing and VDI

We often hear **server-based computing (SBC)** being discussed alongside VDI; so, is this the same technology with a different name or is SBC different in some way?

SBC has been around for quite a long time, and you can actually trace it back as far as the 1950s to mainframe computing. Mainframes were designed to deliver centralized compute power to run applications, with users connecting to the applications using a "green screen" terminal.

Today's SBC model doesn't really change this, but it now offers the ability to connect to either applications or an operating system. We will cover each of these and how they work in the next sections, starting with traditional published application delivery.

Delivering published applications with SBC

So, the first option with SBC is to just deliver an individual application to a user. This is often referred to as publishing an application. The architecture of how this works is shown in the following diagram:

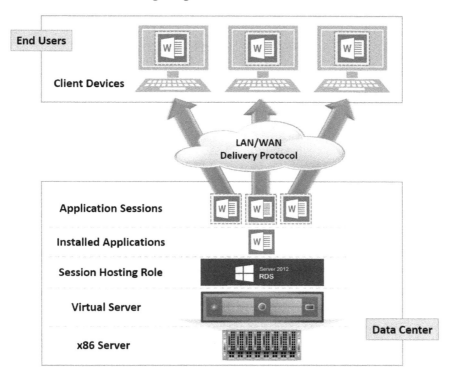

With SBC, rather than connecting to a full-desktop operating system running as a virtual desktop machine, you are now connecting to an application. The application is running on a server; however, it is running in a separate, protected session for each individual user that is connected, which means that a single server can host multiple sessions of the same application for multiple users. The server hosting the application sessions runs a multiuser operating system, and a user would connect to a session using a terminal or thin client. This is why SBC is often referred to as **thin client computing**. SBC has evolved from the mainframe days, and now you can run a desktop operating system as a hosted session, as we will describe in the next section.

Delivering published desktops with SBC

Sometimes, there is a requirement to have a full-desktop experience rather than just having individual applications delivered to the end user. Similar to application publishing, with SBC, you can publish a desktop operating system as a session, as shown in the following diagram:

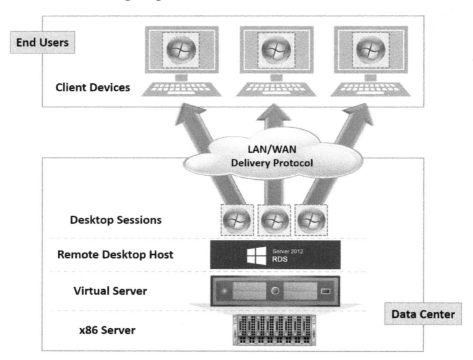

In this model, you are running a desktop operating system rather than an application. The OS runs as a separated, protected session. This is where the differences lie between desktops delivered by SBC and those delivered by VDI.

With VDI, you have a fully functional desktop operating system, on which you can customize, personalize, and install your own applications; whereas with SBC, you are either running just an application session or sharing a desktop environment by having your own session rather than a full desktop.

You also need to bear in mind that in an SBC environment, the desktop session isn't actually running as a true desktop operating system; it is, in fact, running a session of the host servers' operating system, which is made to look like a desktop operating system.

VDI, published applications, or desktop sessions?

So, the question posed in the title of this section is which technology should I choose between VDI, published applications, or perhaps desktop sessions?

There are advantages and disadvantages to all of the above technologies, and ultimately, it will come down to your specific use cases. We will discuss some of the use cases in *Chapter 3*, *Designing and Building a Horizon View 6.0 Infrastructure*.

In most scenarios, it is likely that you will employ a hybrid approach and have a mixed environment of the different technologies. For example, developers might need a full desktop on which they can install applications, so VDI would be suitable for them, whereas a call center operator who only uses one or two applications is more suited to a published application solution.

Horizon View 6.0 can deliver all of these technologies, allowing you to deploy a single platform to manage and deliver the end user experience, no matter what the use case is. In this section, we are just going to cover the VDI elements of Horizon View 6.0, and in the next section, we will highlight some of the benefits of deploying VDI.

The benefits of deploying a VDI solution

With VMware Horizon View 6.0 delivering virtual desktops, you transform your desktop environment into a centrally managed service, enhancing the end user experience and productivity at the same time. At a higher level, Horizon View 6.0 delivers the following:

- **Secure desktop environment**: With centralization, you control your data and deploy policies so that no data leaves the data center, protecting your IP.

- **Centralized management**: Centralizing your desktops as virtual machines not only gives you a central and single point of management, but it also allows for easier operating system or application updates as well as faster deployment of desktop resources.

- **Flexibility and scalability**: This allows you to scale resources up and down quickly as per your business demands, taking into consideration peaks and troughs for seasonal or contract/project-based workers.

- **Mobility and Bring-your-own-device (BYOD)**: This also fits into the flexibility category, but this time allows end users to use devices that suit their needs plus they have the ability to work from anywhere. This also means that organizations don't have the expense of providing employees with hardware, and having to support that hardware.

- **Operational cost savings (OPEX)**: One of the things we hear all the time is that deploying VDI will reduce costs. While that is true, let's be clear that we are talking about operational costs that would potentially be reduced, but sometimes, the capital costs (CAPEX) at the beginning of a VDI project might be higher as you roll out the infrastructure. However, the overall costs over a period of time will reduce through savings in the management of the solution and the fact that you would not be caught in the typical three-year PC refresh cycle trap.

Now that we have talked about what VDI in VMware Horizon View terms is and the differences with SBC, in the next section, we are going to focus on the VMware VDI solution, Horizon View, and take a brief history lesson that covers the background story of where VMware and its VDI story began.

The VMware VDI story

VDI for VMware started back in 2002, when customers of the ESX solution started to virtualize their desktop machines as they had been doing with their server operating systems. There wasn't a specific product or solution at the time and certainly no connection broker or any of the functionality that we see today. All a user had to do was connect to a remote virtual desktop using RDP. That was about as scientific as it got!

It wasn't until 2005 that VMware socialized the idea of having a connection broker for better management of the desktop allocation by demonstrating a prototype at VMworld that year. A company called Propero also showed their version of a connection broker at the same event, and as a result, VDI became more high profile and gained more traction in the market.

Move the clock forward by 2 years to 2007 and you will see that the prototype connection broker was introduced to customers before being given to the product organization to productize it and turn it into a released shipping product called **Virtual Desktop Manager (VDM) 1.0**. This year also saw VMware acquire Propero for $25 million in order to accelerate the connection broker development, leading to the VMworld announcement of VDM 2.0, which was released in January, 2008.

After the release of VDM 2.0 in early 2008, a second release came at the end of the year, along with a new name. **VMware View** had arrived! This year also saw Citrix enter the VDI market with XenDesktop.

A year later, in 2009, VMware View 4.0 was released and was the first version to include the **PCoIP** protocol from Teradici. PCoIP delivered a much richer user experience than RDP.

In 2010, **View 4.5** was released with new features, such as the local mode for delivering offline desktops, PCoIP enhancements, Windows 7 support, and the ability to tier storage. This was also the year that VMware talked publically about the biggest VDI reference case to date with Bank of Tokyo Mitsubishi.

In 2011, the following year, **View 4.6** was released with two new notable features. The first was the iPad client, which allowed a user to connect to their virtual desktop session on an iPad using the PCoIP protocol. The second new feature was the PCoIP Secure Gateway function for the security server, which allowed users to connect to their virtual desktop without needing a VPN connection.

Later on in the same year, **View 5.0** was released with some more new features aimed around the user experience, the key one being the introduction of **Persona Management**, which allowed a user's profile to be independent from the virtual desktop. View 5.0 also introduced 3D graphics support using the latest vSphere 5.0 platform as well as some major overhauls in the PCoIP protocol.

Although it had only a point release in May 2012, **View 5.1** had a number of significant enhancements, especially around storage, with the introduction of the View Storage Accelerator, View Composer Array Integration, and the ability to scale the hosting infrastructure up to a 32-node cluster when using the NFS storage. This version also added RADIUS two-factor authentication, improved the USB device support, standalone View Composer, the ability to support profile migration from XP to Windows 7, and physical desktops with Persona Management.

In March 2013, VMware View 5.2 was released, and to bring it in line with VMware's Horizon branding (launched at the same time), it was renamed **Horizon View 5.2**. In this release, there were a number of new features based on the user experience, such as support for unified communications with Microsoft Lync 2013, hardware-accelerated graphics with **Virtual Shared Graphics Acceleration** (vSGA), and the Windows 8 support. One of the biggest updates came in the form of feature packs, which allowed a user to access their desktop in an HTML 5 browser using the VMware Blast protocol. This feature pack also included the ability to use USB webcams with **Real-Time Audio-Video** (RTAV).

A second release later in 2013 with **Horizon View 5.3** saw the introduction of **virtual dedicated graphics acceleration** (vDGA), which allowed a virtual desktop to have dedicated access to a GPU in the host. This was also the first release that supported Windows Server 2008 R2 as the virtual desktop machine, which means that you can "skin" the operating system to look like a desktop. Finally, the Horizon Mirage support was added to manage full-clone desktops.

The final 5.x release arrived in 2014 with **Horizon View 5.3.1**, adding support for **Virtual SAN** (vSAN).

That brings us nicely up to date—VMware Horizon 6—and a new approach to delivering a fully integrated platform with some new Horizon editions.

The timeline is shown pictorially in the following diagram:

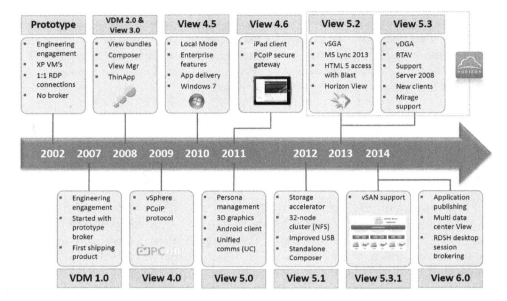

In the next section, we will cover VMware Horizon 6 and the features in each of the different editions in a bit more detail.

An introduction to VMware Horizon 6

In VMware Horizon 6, we have the latest solution in VMware's **end user computing** (**EUC**) vision and strategy for what they describe as *one login, one experience, and any device*. This basically means that for a user, they just need their network password to log in from any device they choose, and once logged in, the look and feel will be consistent across all endpoint devices they use.

We talked earlier about the differences between VDI and SBC and an example use case for application publishing versus VDI versus desktop sessions, and came to the conclusion that a hybrid solution would be the logical way forward. Typically, this would mean that you will need several different product solutions to achieve this; however, with Horizon 6, you can deliver all of this and more, with the ability to deliver VDI, published apps, and session-based desktops—all from a single platform.

Combine this with the other functionalities—such as application virtualization, centralized image management, and automation functionality—and Horizon 6 becomes a compelling solution for delivering all your end user computing needs.

This book is going to focus on the Horizon View 6.0 product and, specifically, how to design, configure, and install the various components for delivering virtual desktops as a centralized service. We will take you on a journey from the initial planning stages right through to the installation, configuration, and optimization.

VMware Horizon 6 was released on 19th June 2014 and comes packaged as "editions" in a similar way to other VMware products, whereby you can buy a bundle of products that make up an entire solution.

In the next section, we will cover the different product editions for Horizon 6.

VMware Horizon 6 editions

As we touched on in the previous section, there are a number of different components that make up the Horizon 6 portfolio, and these features are divided into three different Horizon editions—Standard, Advanced, and Enterprise editions—each building on the functionality of the previous edition.

In the next section, we will take a walk-through of each of the available editions.

Horizon View Standard Edition

Horizon View Standard Edition delivers the core VDI solution and all of its associated features, including the licensing for vSphere and vCenter for desktop. Also included is ThinApp, VMware's application virtualization and packaging solution, which allows you to abstract applications from the underlying operating system and deliver them independent of the OS. You can read more about ThinApp in *VMware ThinApp 4.7 Essentials, Peter Björk, Packt Publishing*.

Horizon Advanced Edition

With Horizon Advanced Edition, we add application publishing, image management, vSAN, and Horizon Workspace.

This is the first edition that includes the application publishing feature that is integrated into Horizon View 6. It allows an application running on a Microsoft RDSH server to be published via the VMware View client using the PCoIP protocol. You can also publish desktop sessions in the same way. For a user, this means that they can access all three delivery methods from one place.

Image management is delivered using **VMware Mirage** with the ability to manage persistent View desktops and also deliver offline desktops to a Mac or Windows laptop. For a detailed overview of VMware Mirage, you can read *VMware Horizon Mirage Essentials, Peter von Oven, Packt Publishing.*

In keeping with the theme of consistent access from one place using any device, Advanced Edition includes the **Horizon Workspace Portal** solution. Horizon Workspace gives an end user their own virtual workspace, which is accessible via a single URL from any device with a compatible browser. Being context-aware, only the applications appropriate for that device and location are shown on the workspace, based on the user's entitlements. Users can also select applications from a central catalog of entitled applications.

Horizon Workspace is sometimes referred to as a universal services broker or the switchboard of the solution. This is because it's the central place you go to in order to access the tools you need, whether that's just an application or a virtual desktop. As it's a universal broker, it's not just about delivering the VMware technology. It allows for the brokering of ThinApp packages, SaaS-based cloud applications, XenApp-published applications, and Microsoft Office 365.

Horizon Enterprise Edition

The final edition is Horizon Enterprise Edition, which builds on the previous two versions and adds features that deliver the operational management and automation functionality. This includes products such as vCenter Operations for View, which delivers capacity planning, health monitoring, and proactive troubleshooting features.

The final component is vCenter Orchestrator with the desktop plugin, which allows you to build desktop workflows for automated provisioning.

The following diagram details the features available in each edition:

	Horizon View	Horizon Advanced	Horizon Enterprise
Management & Automation			
Design & automate workflows(vCO + Desktop Plugin)			☑
Operations Dashboard - Health Monitoring & Perf Analytics (V4V)			☑
Capacity Management - Planning & Optimization (V4V)			☑
Application			
Application Catalog & Brokering – XA, RDSH, SaaS, ThinApp		☑	☑
Application Remoting (RDSH)		☑	☑
Application Packaging & Virtualization (ThinApp)	☑	☑	☑
Desktop Infrastructure			
Virtual Storage (vSAN for Desktop)		☑	☑
Image Management for Physical Desktops (Mirage + Fusion Pro)		☑	☑
Image Management for Virtual Desktops (Mirage for View)		☑	☑
Virtual Desktop Infrastructure (VMware View)	☑	☑	☑
Platform support (vSphere & vCenter for Desktop)	☑	☑	☑

Summary

In this chapter, we discussed what VDI actually is and the different options for delivering the end user experience, compared VDI with desktop and application publishing, and how each solution works. We then wound the clock back to 2002 and looked at the history of where VDI began for VMware.

The final sections covered the latest VMware Horizon 6.0 release and the three different editions—Horizon View Standard, Horizon Advanced, and Horizon Enterprise—and what's included in each edition.

In the next chapter, we are going to start drilling down into the technology a little deeper and look at how some of the technology features included with Horizon View fit together in the overall view and how they work.

2
Horizon View 6.0 Architectural and Feature Overview

In *Chapter 1, Introducing VDI and VMware Horizon 6.0,* we discussed what virtual desktop infrastructure is all about and started to focus on the details of the Horizon View solution. Building on what we learned, this chapter is almost going to act as a glossary or encyclopedia of Horizon View Standard Edition and will introduce you to the architecture and components of the solution.

We will start each section in this chapter with an overview of a specific feature or component, describing its role in the overall solution, how it fits into the infrastructure, and in some cases, take a look under the hood at how it works.

As part of the overall solution, VMware works with a number of third-party vendor technologies that compliment Horizon View, such as antivirus solutions and high-end graphics solutions. These form part of the VMware horizontal solutions and provide reference architectures for various markets such as health care or federal customers.

At the end of this chapter, you will have gained the knowledge that will enable you to describe how Horizon View works, which components perform what tasks, and why you need them.

The Horizon View core components

Let's start this section with a high-level overview of the complete VMware Horizon 6 solution and the components and functionality included in the overall solution, before focusing on the specific Horizon View 6.0 elements of the solution.

It's also probably worth mentioning that as part of the Horizon 6 licensing model, you are licensed to deploy the core hosting infrastructure with the VMware vSphere platform and the vSphere for Desktop license. You can deploy as many ESXi hosts and vCenter servers as you require in order to host only the desktop infrastructure. We will discuss this later in the *The Horizon View Standard Edition licensing* section of this chapter.

The following diagram depicts the Horizon 6 solution and its features:

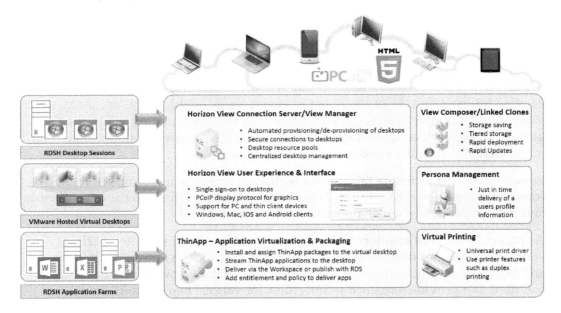

Now that you now have a high-level picture of VMware Horizon 6 and the features it delivers, we are going to take a deeper look into the components that deliver this functionality and how they work in the following sections.

A high-level architecture overview

Overall, the architecture is very straightforward, and for those of you with skills and knowledge of the previous or current versions of VMware, it will be especially so, as Horizon View is hosted on the vSphere platform and leverages the functionality provided by both ESXi and vCenter.

The Horizon View solution builds on the vSphere platform, adding some additional virtual machines that make up the core infrastructure components, such as View Composer and the core to any VDI solution, which is the connection broker.

These additional components are applications that are installed and run on the Microsoft Windows Server operating system (2008 or 2012). They can actually be installed as physical servers; however, the best practice is to virtualize them so that you realize the same benefits as you would while virtualizing any other server.

The following diagram shows you a more detailed overview of the Horizon View architecture, the different components, and how they fit into the solution:

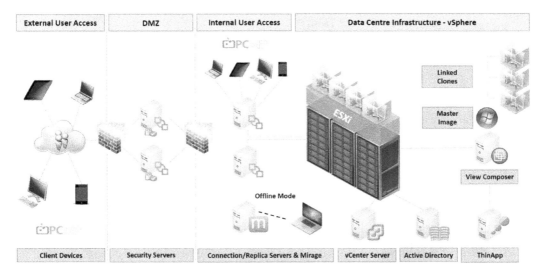

Now here's a question for those of you who have knowledge of previous versions of Horizon View. Have you spotted anything slightly different in the architecture?

Correct! The Transfer Server is no longer a part of Horizon View 6.0 and as such, there is a different way to deliver offline desktops. This way is through deploying VMware Mirage, which can be purchased as a separate product or as part of Horizon Advanced Edition.

In the next sections, we are going to look at each component in more detail.

The Horizon View Connection Server

We will start with the core component of the VMware Horizon View solution, and that's the connection broker or, in VMware terms, the View Connection Server or the View Manager. The Horizon View Connection Server is responsible for connecting the end user to their virtual desktop machine in the data center.

How does it work?

The first contact a user has with Horizon View is when they launch their connection software, called the **Horizon View Client**, or by using a hardware-based integrated PCoIP client and entering their network credentials. We will cover the View Client options in *Chapter 8, Horizon View Clients*. They can also log in using an HTML5-compatible web browser, should they not have the client software. We will cover browser-based access in *Chapter 7, Configuring Horizon View to Deliver Virtual Desktops*.

In the following diagram, we are going to illustrate the login process:

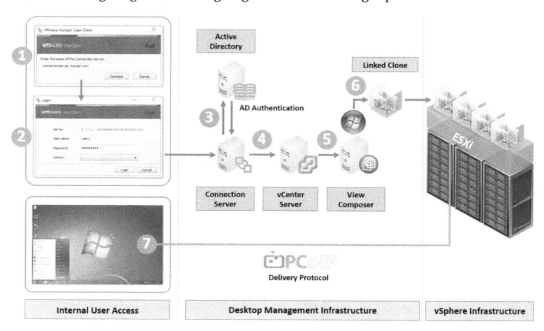

The end user launches their chosen client. In this example, we are going to focus on using the View Client. They enter the details on the connection server (**1**). In response, the connection server requests the user for their login credentials (**2**). The user credentials are basically those that the user would have used when logging in to their physical desktop or any other network application, such as e-mail.

The connection server then authenticates the user credentials against **Active Directory** (**3**), and if it is successful, the user is allowed to continue the login process and gets the option of selecting a desktop to connect to and use.

The desktops they see reflect the Horizon View **desktop pool** that the user is entitled to use. A desktop pool is basically a group of similarly configured virtual desktop machines grouped, for example, on a departmental basis or a specific use case where the pool consists of virtual desktop machines configured in a particular way, maybe for high-end graphics. They might see only one desktop, or they might see several, depending on their entitlement. We will cover managing desktop pools in more detail in *Chapter 7, Configuring Horizon View to Deliver Virtual Desktops*, and discuss the desktop pool design in the next chapter.

Now that it is authenticated, the connection server makes a call to **vCenter Server** (**4**) to start the desktop creation, and then vCenter makes a call to **View Composer** if you are using linked clones (**5**) in order to start the virtual desktop machine build process. We will cover a deep-dive technical overview of linked clones later on in this chapter, in the *Horizon View Composer and linked clones* section.

Linked clone desktops are just one way in which we can create desktops, and we will cover other options in *Chapter 7, Configuring Horizon View to Deliver Virtual Desktops*. We could have provisioned desktops upfront so that they are already available, or you can have your own dedicated virtual desktop machine.

Now that we have our newly created virtual desktop machine (**6**), it is displayed within the View Client using the PCoIP protocol (**7**).

The View connection server is the core component of a VDI solution. It acts as the central broker and is responsible for connecting users to their virtual desktop machine. Ultimately, the broker decides which virtual desktop machine gets assigned to you from a pool and also orchestrates the building of that virtual machine.

The Horizon View security server

The Horizon View security server is another role of the View Connection Server, but architecturally, it sits within your DMZ. The reason for this is that you can allow end users to securely connect to their virtual desktop machine from an external network or the Internet without necessarily needing to connect via a VPN first. The security server does not expose any internal network details to the Internet.

We will cover the installation process of the View security server in *Chapter 4, Installing Horizon View 6.0*, but it's almost identical to installing the View Connection Server. Instead, you select the **View Security Server** option from the drop-down menu of the different role options.

You cannot install a View security server on the same machine that is running a View Connection Server or any of the other Horizon View components.

As part of the installation process, a View security server is *paired* with a View Connection Server on a 1:1 basis, so every security server will be connected to a View Connection Server. This pairing process is configured using a one-time password at the installation time. It's a bit like pairing your Bluetooth phone with the hands-free kit in your car.

We will cover this in the installation of the *Installing the View security server* section in *Chapter 4*, *Installing Horizon View 6.0*.

How does it work?

The login process for the user is the same as when logging in from an internal network; however, there are some different tasks going on in the background, which we will cover later in the chapter.

A user logs in from the View Client, selects a View Connection Server, and enters their login credentials, which are authenticated in Active Directory. So far, the process is no different, but now, the security server elements come into play, as we will now describe.

If the View Connection Server is configured as a PCoIP Gateway, it will pass the connection and address information to the View Client. This connection information allows the View Client to connect to the View security server using PCoIP. This is shown in the following diagram with the green arrow (**1**):

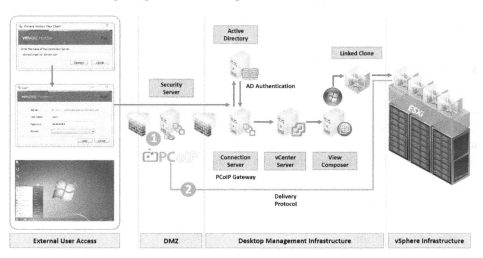

The View security server then forwards the PCoIP connection to the virtual desktop machine (**2**), creating the connection for the user and allowing them to start using it.

The Horizon View replica server

As the name suggests, the Horizon View replica server is exactly that—a replica or copy of the original View Connection Server.

It is used to enable high availability for your Horizon View environment so that if your View Connection Server fails, the replica server takes over and users are still able to connect to their virtual desktop machines.

In line with the security server, the View replica server is another role of the View Connection Server. As you will see in *Chapter 4, Installing Horizon View 6.0*, the installation process is the same as the Connection Server and security server, but this time, you select the replica server role from the drop-down menu.

How does it work?

So, the first question that gets asked is what gets replicated? The View Connection Server stores all its information relating to the end users, desktop pools, and virtual desktop machines in an **Active Directory Application Mode** (**ADAM**) database.

Then, using the **Lightweight Directory Access Protocol** (**LDAP**), which uses a similar method to the Active Directory replication, this View information gets copied from the original View Connection Server to the replica server.

Once the replication has been completed, both the Connection Server and the replica server are now identical to each other. If the View Connection Server fails, you have a backup that steps in and takes over so that end users can still continue to connect to their virtual desktop machines. When the View Connection Server comes back online, the information is replicated so that the two are identical to each other again.

 Just as with the other components, you cannot install the replica server on the same machine that is running a View Connection Server or any of the other Horizon View components.

Horizon View Composer and linked clones

The next component and feature that we are going to discuss is View Composer and what linked clones mean in a desktop environment. We will spend a bit more time concentrating on this subject, as it's a key part of delivering a successful and cost-effective VDI solution. It's also one of those things that often gets confused, so we need to give this subject the justice it deserves.

Let's start with why this is important. An all-too-often reason why a VDI project fails or doesn't even get started comes down to the perceived storage requirements, both from a capacity as well as cost perspective in deploying a storage platform that delivers the performance required for VDI. The reason we see this typically comes down to the fact that the VDI project is being approached in the same way as a physical desktop project would be.

This would mean that each user will get their own dedicated virtual desktop and the hard disk that comes with it, albeit now a virtual disk, but potentially of the same capacity as the desktop PC. It's just like picking the desktop PC up and creating an exact virtualized copy of it in the data center. When you start to scale this to hundreds or maybe even thousands of users, it just doesn't stack up.

We need a new approach to deploy storage in a virtual desktop environment, and that's where the linked clone technology comes into its own.

Linked clones are not only designed to reduce the amount of disk storage space required, but to also make the management and deployment of images to multiple virtual machines a centralized and much easier process.

Introducing the clone technology in Horizon View

Let's start off by defining what we mean by the term **clone**. A clone is an exact copy of an existing virtual desktop machine.

When you create your new clone, it becomes a separate, new virtual desktop machine in its own right, complete with its own unique identity. The cloning process is not a feature of Horizon View; it's actually a function of vSphere and vCenter and works in the same way as cloning server virtual machines. However, with a Horizon View deployment, there is another component to the solution, which is View Composer. View Composer is used to manage the desktop images and the cloning process for the virtual desktop machines. One of the key tasks it performs is the ability to maintain multiple clones.

In our environment, this virtual desktop machine or clone will act as the gold image and will be used as the template from which we can create any new virtual desktop machines.

There are two different types of clone. The first is a **full clone** and the second is a **linked clone**, and we will explain the two types in the following sections.

Full clones

A full clone, as the name suggests, is an exact, full-sized copy of your master image. When you create your clone, the result is a virtual desktop machine that is unique, has its own identity, and has no link to the original master image virtual machine from which it was cloned. It operates as a fully independent virtual desktop machine.

However, one thing to bear in mind is that as it is a full-sized copy, it will consume the same amount of storage as the original parent virtual machine and, therefore, will require greater storage capacity. As we discussed earlier on in this chapter, this might introduce cost implications for deploying VDI due to higher infrastructure costs.

However, before you completely write off the idea of using a full clone, there are actually some use cases that need this model in order to operate. One example is when using VMware Mirage to deliver base layers or application layers. This only works today with a full clone and dedicated virtual desktop machines.

Linked clones

The next method to deploy virtual desktop machines is using the linked clone technology. The idea behind linked clones is that they are based on snapshots and, as a result, will consume far less storage than a full clone.

As this is a key and very important feature of Horizon View, in this section, we will dive deeper into how linked clones work.

The first thing that happens when deploying a linked-clone virtual desktop machine is the creation of a delta disk. This is used by the virtual desktop machine to store the data differences between the newly created virtual desktop machine's own operating system and the operating system of the original gold image or parent virtual desktop machine.

Unlike creating a full-clone disk, the linked-clone disk is not a full copy of the parent image, and this is what defines it as a linked clone. The term linked clone refers to the fact that the linked-clone virtual desktop machine will always refer back to its parent in order to operate. It continues to read from a component called the replica disk. The replica disk is basically a copy of a snapshot of the original parent virtual desktop machine. The original parent virtual desktop machine is then powered off.

The linked clone disk has the potential to grow to the same size as the replica disk if allowed; however, you can set a limit on the size to which it can grow. Should it start to get close to that limit, you can refresh the virtual desktops that are linked to it. This essentially starts the cloning process again from the initial snapshot.

Immediately after a linked clone virtual desktop machine is created, the differences between the parent virtual machine and the newly created virtual desktop machine are extremely small, which means that you don't need the same amount of storage capacity that you would require for a full clone. This is how linked clones are far more space-efficient than their full clone cousins.

If we examine the underlying technology behind linked clones, they are more like snapshots than they are clones, but with one key difference; this is where View Composer comes in. View Composer allows you to have more than one active snapshot linked to the parent virtual machine disk, ideal for a desktop environment, as you will be creating multiple virtual desktop machines.

The best practice would be to deploy an environment with linked clones so as to reduce the storage requirements; however, as we previously mentioned, there are some use cases where you will need to use full clones.

One thing we need to highlight while on the subject of storage is that rather than capacity, we are now talking about the storage performance of your entire VDI environment.

If we start with linked clones, all of your linked-clone virtual desktop machines are going to be reading from only one replica, and therefore, it's important to host the replica on a fast storage that can deliver the number of IOPS required. Depending on your desktop pool design, you will probably have more than one replica and typically more than one datastore. We will cover storage sizing in more detail in *Chapter 3, Designing and Building a Horizon View 6.0 Infrastructure*, apart from best practices on where to host the replica and the types of disk to use.

When it comes to storage acceleration technologies, it's useful to remember that Horizon View has its own integrated solution called the **View Storage Accelerator (VSA)** or **Content Based Read Cache (CBRC)**. This feature allows you to allocate up to 2 GB of memory from the ESXi host server that is hosting your virtual desktop machines to be used as a cache that contains the most commonly read blocks.

In a VDI environment, we are talking about booting up a desktop operating system and, therefore, there will be a lot of duplication of required blocks. These can now be retrieved from the memory in order to accelerate the process.

In addition to the VMware integrated options, there are also a number of other third-party solutions that deliver storage acceleration and optimization technologies, such as Atlantis Computing and their ILIO products—Nutanix, Nimble, and Tintri, to name a few.

One thing that needs to be mentioned before you start looking at any of these technologies for VDI is to first look at your physical desktop assessment data and understand your current desktop storage performance and requirements. We will cover this in *Chapter 3*, *Designing and Building a Horizon View 6.0 Infrastructure*. You might find that you don't actually require additional storage solutions.

An alternative solution can be to use the **View Composer Array Integration (VCAI)**, which allows the process of building linked clones to be offloaded to the storage array rather than taking CPU cycles from your ESXi host server.

Having now described the different types of clones you can create, the next section will take an in-depth look into how linked clones work.

How do linked clones work?

Before you start any form of cloning, the first thing you need to do is to create your virtual desktop machine that will be used as the parent virtual machine or gold master image. This should contain the operating system, core applications, and other settings. You will also need to install the Horizon View Agent components.

We will cover the desktop image-building process in more detail in *Chapter 7*, *Configuring Horizon View to Deliver Virtual Desktops*.

Now that we have built our image, we will use it to create any new subsequent virtual desktop machines.

An overview of the linked clone process is shown in the following diagram:

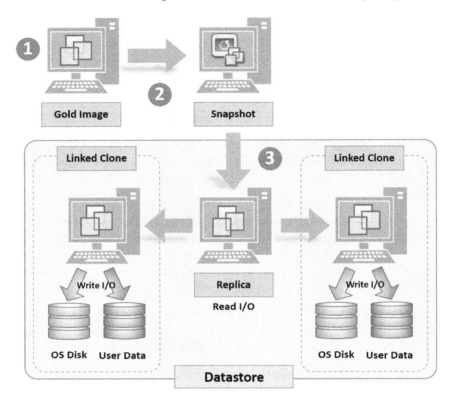

Once you have created your **Gold Image** (1) or—as it's referred to in VMware terms—the **Parent Image**, you take a snapshot (2). When you create your desktop pool, this snapshot is selected and becomes the **Replica** (3) and will be set to be read-only. Each virtual desktop machine will be linked back to this replica, and hence the term linked clone.

 Try not to create too many snapshots for your Parent VM. Just have one or no more than a handful, otherwise this could impact the performance of your desktops and make management a bit harder, determining the snapshots.

What does View Composer build?

During the virtual desktop machine build process and once the replica disk has been created, View Composer creates a number of other virtual disks as well as the linked clone (OS disk) itself. We will explain these different disks in the following sections.

The linked-clone disk

Not wanting to state the obvious, the main disk that gets created is the linked-clone disk itself. This disk is basically an empty virtual disk container that gets attached to the virtual desktop machine, as the user logs in and the desktop starts up.

As we have already discussed, this disk will start off small in size but will grow over time, depending on the block changes that are requested from the replica disk by the virtual desktop machines operating system. These block changes are stored in the linked-clone disk, and this is why this disk is sometimes referred to as the delta disk or differential disk. This is due to the fact that it stores all the delta changes that the desktop operating system requests from the replica disk. The linked-clone disk can only grow to the maximum size of its parent; however, you should never let that happen. Typically, it will only grow to a couple of hundred MBs. We will cover this in the *The linked-clone process* section later.

The replica disk is set as read-only and is used as the primary disk. Any writes and/or block changes that are requested by the virtual desktop are written/read directly from the linked clone disk.

 It is a recommended best practice to allocate tier 1 storage, such as local SSD drives, to host the replica, as all virtual desktops will be using a single read-only VMDK file as their base image.

The persistent disk or user data disk

The persistent disk feature of View Composer allows you to configure a separate disk that contains just the user data and user settings separate from the operating system. This allows any user data to be preserved when you update or make changes to the operating system disk, as we will see when we cover some of the other linked clones features.

This disk is also used to store the user profiles. You need to size this disk accordingly in order to ensure that it is large enough to store the user profiles, especially when using roaming profiles. This is another reason why it's a good idea to run a desktop assessment so that you can build a picture of your desktop user environment, in order to understand what users are doing and what they require.

The disposable disk

The disposable disk option, as the name suggests, allows Horizon View to create a temporary disk that is deleted when the user powers off their virtual desktop machine.

If you think about how the Windows operating system works and the files that it creates, there are several files that are only required on a temporary basis—files such as temporary Internet files or the Windows pagefile, for example. As these are only temporary files, why would you want to keep them and take up storage space unnecessarily?

Horizon View provides the option to have a disposable disk for each virtual desktop that can be used to store these temporary files, which will be deleted on power off.

One thing to point out here is that we are talking about temporary system files and not user files. A user's temporary files are still stored on the user data disk so that they are preserved. Having said that, you might want to delete the temporary user data, in which case, you can redirect the temporary user files to the disposable disk.

The internal disk

Finally, we have the internal disk. The internal disk is used to store important configuration information such as the computer account password, which would be required to join the virtual desktop machine to the domain if you performed a refresh operation. It is also used to store Sysprep and QuickPrep configuration details. We will cover what QuickPrep is in *Chapter 7, Configuring Horizon View to Deliver Virtual Desktops*.

In terms of disk space, the internal disk is relatively small at only 20 MB. By default, the user will not see this disk from their Windows Explorer, as it contains important configuration information that you wouldn't want them to delete.

The following diagram shows you an outline of the different disk types created:

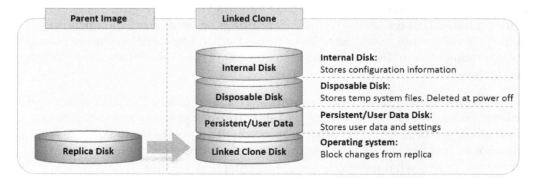

The linked-clone process

So, now that we have covered what View Composer does, let's look at how the process for building a linked clone virtual desktop machine works and what goes on under the hood.

When a user logs into Horizon View and requests a virtual desktop machine, which is View Manager, in conjunction with the vCenter Server and View Composer, will start the process to create the virtual desktop machine. There are three key stages to this process:

- Create
- Build
- Customize

This process is detailed in the following diagram:

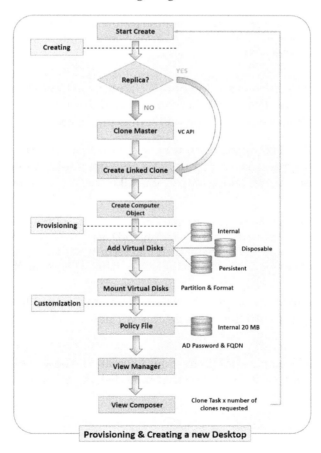

Now that we have covered the build process for linked clones, there are a number of tasks that we can perform in order to manage and update the linked clone and the virtual desktop image.

The linked-clone features and functions

There are a number of functions that you can perform on linked clones in order to deliver the ongoing management of the virtual desktop machines.

The recompose operation

Recomposing a linked-clone virtual desktop machine allows you to perform updates to the operating system disk, such as updating the image with the latest patches or software updates.

> You can only update the same version of an operating system. You cannot use the recompose feature to migrate from one operating system to another, for example, migrating from Windows XP to Windows 7.

As we covered in the previous section of this chapter, we have separate disks for things such as user data. These disks are not affected during a recompose operation, which means that all user-specific data on them is preserved.

When you initiate the recompose operation, View Composer essentially starts the linked-clone-building process over again, so a new operating system disk is created, which then gets customized, and a snapshot is taken, as we previously described.

> During the recompose operation, the MAC address of the network card and the Windows SID are not preserved. There are some management tools and security solutions that might not work due to this change. The UUID will remain the same.

Before you start the recompose process, the first thing you need to do is update your parent master image (1) with the patch updates or new applications that you want to deploy.

The next step is to take a snapshot (2) in order to create the new replica (3). The existing operating system disk is destroyed. The user data disk (4) is maintained during the recompose process.

This is shown in the following diagram with the old version on the left-hand side and the newly recomposed linked clone shown on the right-hand side of the diagram:

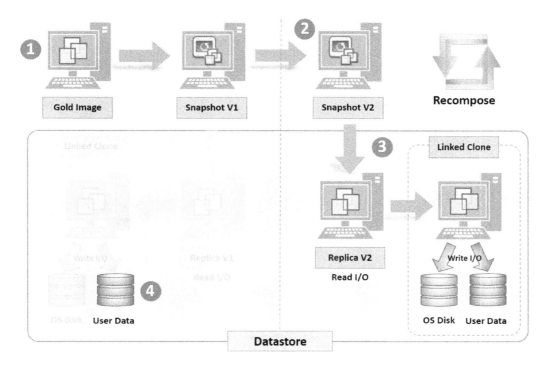

The refresh operation

By initiating a refresh of the linked-clone virtual desktop machine, you are effectively carrying out a factory restore, reverting it back to how it was on day one, and its original snapshot that was taken after it had completed the customization phase.

This refresh operation only applies to the operating system disk, and none of the other disks are affected.

So, why would you need to refresh the linked-clone virtual desktop machine? One of the main reasons why you would perform this operation is because the operating system disk starts to become full. We have already discussed the fact that the operating system disk can grow to be the full size of its parent image.

This is also good for VDI environments that are in public areas so that nothing gets left behind on the virtual desktop machine when the user logs out. The next user gets a completely fresh machine.

This means that it would be taking up more disk space than is really necessary, which kind of defeats the objective of having linked clones in the first place. By performing a refresh operation and essentially resetting the linked clone back to the original snapshot, it will revert to having only a small delta between itself and its parent image, and therefore, takes up less storage space.

The following diagram shows you a representation of the refresh operation:

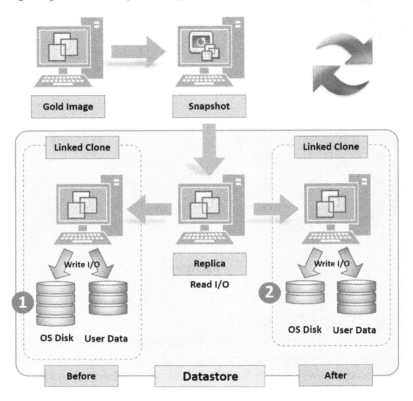

The linked clone on the left-hand side of the diagram (**1**) has started to grow in size. Performing the refresh operation reverts it to the snapshot as if it were a new virtual desktop, as shown on the right-hand side of the diagram (**2**).

The rebalance operation

The rebalance operation is used to evenly distribute the linked-clone virtual desktop machines across the multiple datastores you might have in your Horizon View environment. You would perform a rebalance if one of your datastores was nearing capacity and others had ample free space.

This might also help with the performance of that particular datastore. For example, if you had 10 virtual desktop machines in one datastore and only two in another, running a rebalance operation would potentially even this out, leaving you with six virtual desktop machines per datastore. The following diagram describes the rebalance operation:

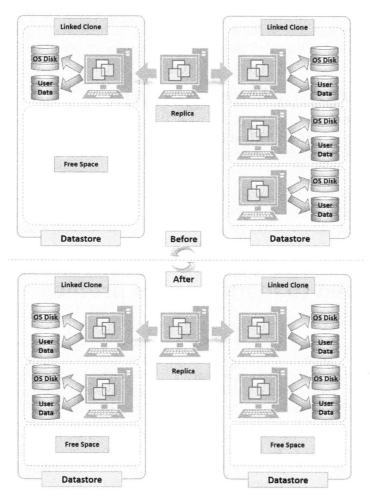

 You must use the View Administrator management console to initiate the rebalance operation in View Composer. We will cover the View Administrator in more detail in *Chapter 5, A Guided Tour of the Horizon View Administrator Console*. If you simply try to vMotion any of your virtual desktop machines, View Composer will not be able to keep track of them.

On the other hand, if you had six virtual desktop machines on one datastore and seven on another, it is highly likely that initiating a rebalance operation will have no effect and no virtual desktop machines will be moved.

A virtual desktop machine will only be moved to another datastore if the target datastore has significantly more spare capacity than the source.

Now we have covered linked clones in some detail. In the next section, we are going to cover some of the other core components and features of Horizon View.

View Persona Management

Starting with a little bit of background, View Persona Management was originally a technology product called Virtual Profiles, which was acquired by VMware from the company that produced it, which is RTO Software, back in 2010. It's designed to manage user profiles within a virtualized desktop environment.

VMware View Persona Management was first released with View 5.0 and allows you to configure a user's profile so that it dynamically synchronizes with a remote profile repository on a file server in the data center. It's a standard component and is part of the VMware View Standard Edition license.

Do we need to manage user profiles differently?

In short, yes we do, due to the way in which we can now manage the delivery of a virtual desktop machine and the fact that a user might not own their desktop, and we have a floating pool of desktop resources from which a user can be assigned any virtual desktop machine. If we have a dedicated desktop assigned to a user, we might not need this option. Let's explain what this means.

In a VDI solution, one of the key benefits of lowering infrastructure requirements and management overheads is the way in which the virtual desktops are built, either on demand or delivered from a pool of prebuilt, floating, or stateless desktops, as they are commonly referred to. The typical deployment model is the stateless desktop model, whereby the user doesn't actually own their desktop, they are merely borrowing it, and once they have finished with it, it goes back into a pool for somebody else to borrow.

Stateless refers to the fact that all desktops start as a Vanilla-built, unpersonalized desktop, which gets customized to the user as they use it. However, once they log out, it returns back to its Vanilla state, ready for the next user.

Using this stateless model will require some tools or solutions that deliver the personalization elements to the virtual desktop machine.

This is where View Persona Management comes into play. It delivers the user's profile to the virtual desktop machine that they have been assigned to, effectively making it theirs.

Earlier, we touched on the subject of the desktop being built on demand; so, what does this mean exactly? What we are referring to is how the desktop is put together from several different component parts. The desktop can be broken down into three key component parts: an operating system, applications, and the user profile; the latter is the bit that makes it yours, if you like.

In a VDI solution, it makes sense to separate these parts so that we can deliver them back to any desktop that gets allocated to the user, which means that we can take advantage of having a pool of floating desktops, and ultimately, having less virtual machines than the number of users. This is what is referred to as concurrency. We will talk more about this in *Chapter 3, Designing and Building a Horizon View 6.0 Infrastructure*.

As a user logs on, these pieces all come together to deliver the end user desktop experience. In this section, we are talking about the View Persona Management and delivering a user's profile. This is shown in the following diagram:

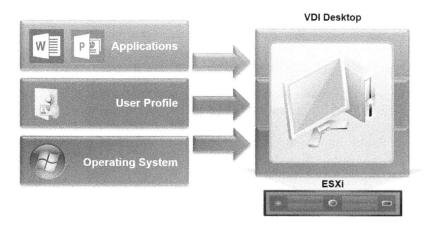

The benefits of using View Persona Management

At a high level, View Persona Management provides the following features:

- Just-in-time retrieval of a user's profile from their virtual desktop
- No infrastructure—just a file share or existing folder redirection structure
- Driven by Active Directory Group Policy
- Maintains personalization between sessions
- No dependency on Windows roaming user profiles
- Support for Windows XP, Windows Vista, Windows 7, and Windows 8.x

As we previously mentioned, one of the key reasons for using View Persona Management is that you can deploy more stateless virtual desktop machines to lower the infrastructure and management costs.

Printing from a Horizon View Virtual Desktop

A question that often comes up when deploying a VDI solution is how you manage printing. As your virtual desktop machine is now running on a server in the data center, when you hit the print button, where does your print job come out? What about printer drivers; which ones do I install? Typically, your desktop has the driver installed for the printer that is nearest to you or for a locally attached printer. Does this mean that you need to install every printer driver possible onto your virtual desktop machines? Luckily, the answer to these questions is no.

Bundled within Horizon View is an OEM virtual printing solution, called ThinPrint, from a company called Cortado that works with the PCoIP protocol. ThinPrint allows your end users to print to either a network printer or to a local printer that is attached via USB and that uses the USB redirection feature of View to connect the printer from the user's endpoint device to their virtual desktop machine. The USB device management is covered in the next section.

So to answer the questions we raised at the beginning of this section around the printer drivers to install, ThinPrint uses a single virtual print driver that replaces all other print drivers. You can still install a specific print driver, if required, for use cases where your printer has some additional features or functionality; however, the virtual print driver has support for most multifunctional printers, supporting features such as double-sided printing.

The other question was on the location and where your print job actually gets printed. This is addressed with the location-based printing feature that allows you to map to a printer that is nearest to your endpoint device.

There are two key components of the virtual printing solution that get installed as part of the Horizon View installation process. These two components are as follows:

- **The .print Engine**: This gets installed on the virtual desktop machine as part of the Horizon View Agent installation and also includes the virtual print driver

- **The .print Client**: This gets installed on the endpoint device as part of the Horizon View Client and provides information on the available printers as well as receives the print jobs from the engine component

Managing USB devices in a virtual desktop

We are all used to plugging USB devices such as memory sticks into our laptops and desktops, but now that your desktop is a virtual desktop machine, how do you continue to use your USB devices? Horizon View has the ability to redirect your USB device from the physical endpoint into which you plug the USB device to your virtual desktop machine using the PCoIP protocol. The USB device appears as if it's connected to the virtualized desktop and will appear in the device manager, for example. Don't forget, you will still need to have the drivers installed for this device if Windows cannot detect them.

USB device support in Horizon View

There isn't an exhaustive list of devices that work within Horizon View, as that would be a very long list.

In general, most devices should work, as all that Horizon View is doing is redirecting the USB traffic from the View Client on the endpoint device to the View Agent running on the virtual desktop machine. There could well be some devices that don't work purely due to the nature of the device itself, for example, security devices that check the endpoint they are plugged into. We used to classify USB webcams in this category; however, with the introduction of **Real-Time Audio-Video (RTAV)**, most of these devices can now be supported. We will cover this later on in this chapter.

One of the things that often gets raised is around security and the fact that you wouldn't want to allow people to plug USB memory sticks into their virtual desktop machines. In the next section, we will talk about how you can select the USB devices that you can connect to the virtual desktop machine using the USB filtering feature.

Filtering supported USB devices

As we just highlighted, you might not want to allow users to have the ability to plug in external USB devices and redirect them to their virtual desktop in some circumstances.

Horizon View has a feature that can prevent USB devices from being redirected to a virtual desktop machine. You can apply this using a policy on the endpoint device, the virtual desktop, or using an Active Directory Group Policy. For example, you might want to prevent USB memory sticks from being used.

You can create specific filters to include devices that you want to allow but block others, so if you have a corporate standard device, this would be allowed. You can even go to the next level of detail and choose a particular model of device from a specific vendor but block any other devices even though they are from the same vendor.

Managing multifunction USB devices

You might also have some USB devices that have several different functions in your environment but within a single device with a single USB connection. For example, a multimedia keyboard can have a touchpad mouse, speakers, a fingerprint reader, as well as the keyboard itself.

Horizon View supports a function known as device splitting. This allows you to just redirect certain components of the device rather than the entire device. With our multimedia keyboard example, you might want to leave the mouse as a local device on the endpoint device, while redirecting the fingerprint reader to allow a secure logon to the virtual desktop machine.

ThinApp application virtualization

As part of the Horizon View Standard Edition license, ThinApp is also included. Discussing ThinApp in great detail is a whole book in itself, so in this section, we are just going to skim the surface and give you a very high-level overview of the product.

ThinApp is an application virtualization or application-packaging solution that abstracts applications from the underlying operating systems, which is a bit like how a hypervisor decouples an operating system from the physical hardware. However, now we have moved up a level and are looking at separating applications from the operating systems.

So, why do I need ThinApp?

It's designed to eliminate the application conflict and streamline the application delivery and management. One of the key use cases is to deliver applications that might not run or be supported on your operating system version.

An example of this is running Internet Explorer 6 on Windows 7, where IE6 will only run on Windows XP. However, by packaging IE6 as a ThinApp, I can now run it on Windows 7 without any problems. In the next section, we will cover how it does this.

What is ThinApp application virtualization?

ThinApp encapsulates applications into a single package consisting of a single .exe or .msi file and abstracts them from:

- The host operating system
- Any traditionally installed applications already running on the system
- All other virtual applications running on the system

Applications are run in a virtual environment and have minimal or zero impact on the underlying operating system.

When you create a ThinApp package, you are capturing all the application files, registry settings, and filesystems that an application requires in order to execute. It also captures its own agent as part of the process so that the end client requires nothing to be installed.

Once packaged, the application can be deployed (either streamed or installed) onto the virtual desktop machine or even a physical desktop.

 ThinApp packages can only execute on a Windows operating system, whether it's a physical PC or virtual desktop machine.

When running a ThinApp application, it's important to note that the package makes no changes to the operating system of the machine that it's running on.

There are no requirements for backend infrastructure either. All your ThinApp packaged applications are stored in a file share on a file server. This means that you can centrally manage and update your packages so that all users will receive the updates the next time they launch the application.

For a detailed look at ThinApp, you can read *VMware ThinApp 4.7 Essentials, Peter Björk, Packt Publishing.*

Antivirus for virtual desktop machines

Let's start by looking at a traditional desktop antivirus scanning model where an agent is installed and runs on every desktop in the environment. The job of the agent is to perform the antivirus scan and also update the definition file that contains information on the latest malware.

For a desktop PC environment, this model works well, but in a VDI infrastructure, there will be a few challenges. When a scan starts on every virtual desktop, its resource usage will significantly increase, but if you think about the VDI model, these desktops are running on a single ESXi host server, and it's the server that will buckle.

For example, you had a host server running 100 virtual desktop machines, and at 12 p.m. on a Thursday afternoon, they all kicked off a virus scan. This host is likely to become 100 percent utilized very quickly, both for the CPU and storage I/O. The result will be unresponsive desktops. Instead of affecting one user's desktop, you have now affected all 100. You can look at scheduling the scans so that they are staggered, but it's not just the scanning that can cause issues.

Taking into consideration what we have discussed so far in having stateless desktops, if you are recomposing desktops or building on demand, you now have to download the definitions file to the virtual desktop machine every time, taking up valuable network bandwidth and storage capacity.

A final consideration is the memory footprint of the AV software that you install on each of the virtual desktop machines. Typically, you will need more available memory in order to run the agents and scanning process.

With VMware vSphere 5.5, we have a new approach with a product called vShield Endpoint, which is included in the license. In a Horizon View deployment, vShield Endpoint consolidates and offloads all antivirus operations into one centralized location in the form of a **security virtual appliance (SVA)**.

VMware has partnered with antivirus software vendors to supply the dedicated SVA that integrates with the vShield Endpoint interface to protect virtual desktop machines against viruses and other malware. Now, rather than installing an antivirus agent onto each individual virtual desktop machine, you connect to the SVA instead. Architecturally, you will deploy one SVA per ESXi host.

VMware works with a number of partners who deliver an SVA appliance for vShield Endpoint, such as Bitdefender, Kaspersky, McAfee, Symantec, and Trend Micro.

The VMware vShield Endpoint architecture

As we discussed previously, instead of installing the antivirus software on each virtual desktop machine, you install the SVA from your chosen vendor. You will need one SVA per ESXi host server, as shown in the following diagram of the architecture:

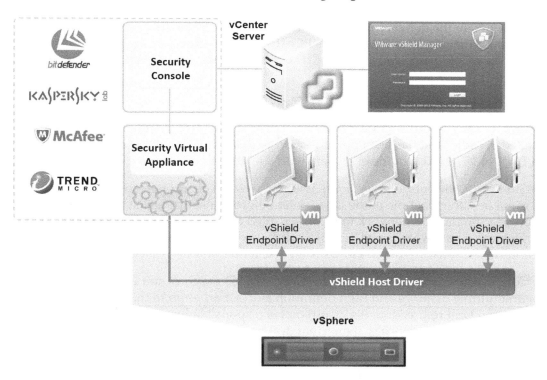

Rather than having to install an agent on each virtual desktop machine to be protected, you only need a small-footprint vShield Endpoint driver. This driver is part of the VMware Tools installation for the virtual desktop machine.

This means that if you were to switch to a different antivirus vendor, you don't need to install a new agent onto every virtual desktop. You simply deploy your new SVA. IT administrators centrally manage VMware vShield Endpoint with the vShield Manager console, which then integrates with VMware vCenter Server.

The PCoIP protocol – delivering the desktop experience

So far, we have really only talked about building the virtual desktop machines and some of the features that help you build a solid infrastructure, but the most important task in any VDI solution is how do you get the screen contents of the virtual desktop machine running in the data center delivered to the users endpoint device you are remotely connecting from.

This is where the delivery protocol comes in. VMware Horizon View 6, like previous versions, uses **PC-over-IP** (**PCoIP**). In this section, we are going to cover what the PCoIP protocol is and how it works to deliver the end user experience.

An introduction to PCoIP

PCoIP is a high-performance, UDP-based display protocol designed by a company called Teradici and has been purpose-built to deliver virtual desktop machines over a LAN or WAN to provide end users with a feature-rich desktop experience.

With PCoIP, the entire screen content is compressed, encrypted, and encoded on the virtual desktop machine in the data center before transmitting just the pixels, either across a standard IP network to PCoIP-enabled endpoint devices such as zero clients, which use a hardware-based Teradici solution, or a Windows, Mac, or a tablet device running the software-based Horizon View Client.

PCoIP supports high resolution, full-frame rate 3D graphics and HD media, along with multiple displays and high definition audio. Earlier on in this chapter, we discussed USB redirection. It's PCoIP that is responsible for redirecting USB devices from the endpoint device to the virtual desktop machine.

PCoIP was designed and built from the ground up specifically to deliver a full desktop experience. Being a dynamic protocol, PCoIP ensures the best user experience regardless of whether the user is connecting via a LAN or WAN. It can dynamically adapt based on the network conditions, available bandwidth, and the end user policy.

The quality of the image that PCoIP delivers can be controlled via a group policy in order to allow you to deliver the appropriate image quality depending on the use case. The image is built progressively from what is called a perceptually lossless image to a completely lossless image, with the latter delivering a pixel perfect image. For example, would you really need to build a pixel-perfect image if you were just running Microsoft Outlook?

Other protocols – Remote Desktop Protocol

RDP was developed by Microsoft and is used primarily to connect to a remote machine—either a server, desktop, or virtual machine—using TCP/IP. RDP is now more commonly known as the Remote Desktop Connection, and you probably use it on a daily basis to connect to your server infrastructure remotely.

What are the key differences between PCoIP and RDP?

Now that we have an understanding of PCoIP and RDP, why should we choose PCoIP?

One of the key reasons is that as it's built using a UDP protocol rather than TCP, UDP as a protocol is better suited for delivering real-time data such as streaming. This in itself lends it to the VDI model in a better manner. If you think about the two protocols, you can see why.

UDP is used to get the data to the endpoint device as quickly as possible, which is exactly what you need for virtual desktops. With TCP, it's all about how the data is being received and whether it has arrived successfully. If not all the data packets are received, TCP will ask for the transmission to either slow down or stop completely. This slowing down results in poor performance for the end user, and they might experience jerky or choppy display behavior from their virtual desktop.

A UDP-based protocol just keeps sending data and is much speedier simply because there is no acknowledgement from the endpoint device.

PCoIP is also far more configurable, especially when it comes to the bandwidth usage. It allows you to configure the image quality depending on the use case and what the user is doing. Bandwidth is usually the root cause in most display-related issues within a virtual desktop infrastructure.

The dynamic nature of PCoIP, when it comes to the available bandwidth, helps when there are constraints on the network. If there is ample bandwidth available, it can deliver the best experience possible with high quality images, but when there is network congestion, it can turn down the image quality until the bandwidth becomes available again.

However, there are still some cases where PCoIP won't be the appropriate protocol to use. The main one we see most of the time is with network ports being blocked. When you connect to your Horizon View session with the View Client, you initiate the connection on port 443. When your desktop is displayed back to you, PCoIP will use UDP port 4172 to send the pixels. This port is blocked sometimes, as it's not typically used for anything else. The result of this port being blocked is that even though you will be able to log on to your virtual desktop via the View Client and everything looks okay, you will just receive a black screen. The black screen is due to the pixels being blocked as they are sent. In this scenario, the workaround is to access the desktop from an HTML5-enabled browser. We will cover this in *Chapter 9, Fine-tuning the End User Experience*.

In the next section, we are going to look at how we can deliver an even higher level of graphics capabilities.

Hardware-accelerated graphics in Horizon View

Before we get into the fine details, let's start with a brief background of the high-end graphic features in Horizon View.

The support for high-end graphics has been released in phases, with the first phase supporting 3D graphics, which shipped with vSphere 5 and View 5.0, using a software-based rendering solution. This allowed support for Windows Aero, for example, but was still not up for some of the real high-end use cases such as CAD applications.

If we had been having this conversation previously, and you had a use case that required high-end graphics capabilities, virtual desktops at that time would not have been a viable solution. As we just discussed, in a VDI environment, graphics would be delivered using software. We are also using the graphics card on the server, which typically has limited capabilities, as all it needs to do is show a local console.

In the next phase, a hardware-based GPU solution was released with vSphere 5.1, allowing the host servers to make use of a physical GPU card to process graphics, which in turn allowed the virtual desktop machines to take advantage of physical GPU features from the card installed in the host server, as we will see later in this section.

Now that the hypervisor supports physical GPU cards, with the release of View 5.2 back in 2013, the ability to deliver hardware-accelerated graphics capabilities became a standard product feature with the introduction of **Virtual Shared Graphics Acceleration (vSGA)**, which was then followed with the launch of **Virtual Dedicated Graphics Acceleration (vDGA)**.

We will discuss these two technologies in the upcoming sections of this chapter and also touch on the next installment of graphics capabilities in Horizon View with the announcement of **Virtual Graphics Processing Unit (vGPU)**.

Virtual Shared Graphics Acceleration

vSGA allows for multiple virtual desktop machines to share a physical GPU card that is installed into the ESXi host server that hosts the virtual desktop machines.

In this model, the virtual desktop machines do not have direct, dedicated access to the physical GPU card and, instead, work by using the VMware SVGA 3D graphics driver that is installed on each virtual desktop operating system. The SVGA is a VMware driver that provides support for DirectX 9.0c and OpenGL 2.1.

Graphic commands from the virtual desktop machines are captured by the SVGA driver and directed to the hypervisor that controls the GPU. In this configuration, the NVIDIA driver is installed on vSphere and not the virtual desktop machines' operating system. In later vSphere and ESX versions, VMware now supports AMD cards too.

The following diagram shows you an overview of the vSGA architecture:

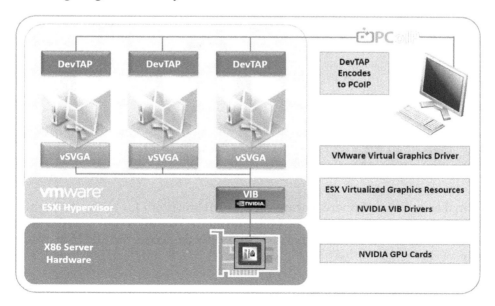

The advantage of vSGA is that you can host more virtual desktop machines per host; however, it might still not offer the high-end capabilities that some users might require. For this, you might need vDGA, which we will cover in the next section.

Virtual Dedicated Graphics Acceleration

With vDGA, you can give an individual virtual desktop machine dedicated access directly to a physical GPU card in the ESXi host server.

Adopting this model allows the virtual desktop machine to make full use of the capabilities of the GPU, making it perfect for such use cases where the end user runs engineering applications or CAD systems. vDGA supports all the native NVIDIA functions, such as NVIDIA CUDA, DirectX 9, 10, and 11, as well as OpenGL 4.4.

The following diagram shows you the architecture for vDGA:

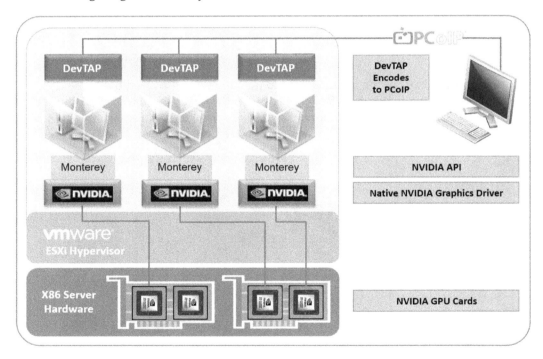

vDGA makes use of a vSphere feature called VMDirectPath I/O pass-through, which is sometimes referred to as PCI pass-through. This allows the virtual desktop machine to "pass through" the hypervisor and directly access the GPU hardware in the host server.

As a virtual desktop machine is mapped directly to a GPU on a one-to-one basis, you cannot use vSphere features such as HA, DRS, or vMotion, which you can take advantage of with the vSGA model.

Unified communications support

In a fashion similar to the high-end graphics support, if we had been having a conversation about running unified communications or a VoIP session on a VDI desktop previously, I would have described it as kryptonite for VDI! It just didn't work.

The first call might have been acceptable; however, adding more users would ultimately result in resource-constrained servers that can no longer operate due to the amount of traffic generated. This would mean that the call experience would have been unusable.

However, all that has now changed, and you can now deploy a unified communications solution on your virtual desktop machines. There was always a great use case for this solution and VDI in, for example, a call center environment where you can deliver a DR solution or allow users to work from home if they are unable to make it to the office.

So why exactly didn't it work? Other than the fact that unified communication vendors didn't support it, it was quite simply because when you placed a VoIP call from your virtual desktop, the voice and video data goes through the virtual desktop, through the data center infrastructure, and eventually to the person you were calling. This would not only cause bandwidth issues making your desktop unresponsive, but also mean fewer virtual desktop machines per host due to the amount of additional processing they would need to manage, putting additional load on the servers in the data center.

With the introduction of an API and the communication vendor software supporting this API, media is now encoded and decoded on the client device rather than going via the data center. This also fixes the consolidation issue of the reduced number of virtual desktop machines per host.

To solve these issues and produce a working solution, VMware concentrated on three key areas delivering the following features:

- Offloading media processing to the client device — removing the load that was placed on the server in the data center

- Optimized point-to-point media delivery, eliminating the hairpin effect.
- High quality UC VoIP and Video with QoS.

The following diagram shows you the before and after of unified communications in virtual desktops:

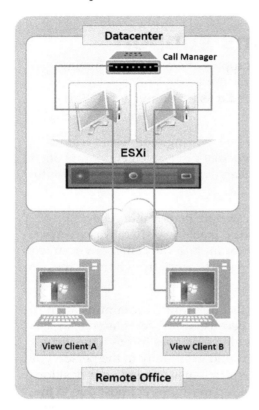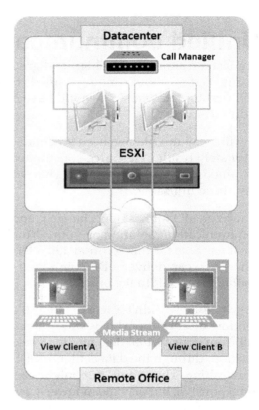

Support for Microsoft Lync 2013

VMware has worked with Microsoft to provide a fully certified solution to deploy Microsoft Lync 2013 in a Horizon View virtual desktop machine. This includes full support for VoIP and video using the PCoIP protocol.

To enable Lync, you need to ensure that your endpoint device has the Lync VDI plugin installed along with the View Client and the Microsoft Lync 2013 Client. As part of the collaboration, VMware has implemented Microsoft's **dynamic virtual channels** (**DVC**) inside PCoIP. DVC provides the communication path between the virtual desktop machine and endpoint device.

Real-Time Audio-Video

In keeping with the theme of communications, the next question that comes up is the support for using a USB webcam with a virtual desktop machine.

The issue

Previously, this provided the same challenges as we saw with unified communications and VoIP. Using a webcam or devices using audio in a virtual desktop machine was not supported due to the high bandwidth requirements these types of device require. As the redirection of these types of devices was handled with the USB redirection feature of the PCoIP protocol, the traffic was sent over the same protocol as your desktop, slowing your desktop down.

The other part of the issue is that the audio to the endpoint also travelled down the same tunnel as the USB webcam traffic and the desktop, just adding to the bandwidth issues. As for audio-in, well that never worked at all!

A part of the problem is that you can't separate audio-in from audio-out when using a USB audio device. This means that using a USB headset for a VoIP call required the entire headset to be forwarded to the guest, yet more bandwidth was required.

How does RTAV fix this issue?

RTAV does not forward audio and webcam devices using the USB redirection function of the PCoIP protocol. Instead, the devices are left local to the endpoint and audio/images are pulled from the local devices. The audio/images are then encoded, delivered to the virtual desktop machine, and decoded.

Now, in the device manager of the virtual desktop machine, you will also see that a virtual webcam and a virtual microphone have been installed.

RTAV supports:

- Webcams and audio-in at the same time for VoIP video conference applications such as Google Talk and Skype
- Audio-in only (without video) for VoIP calls
- Webcam for webcam monitoring applications or taking photographs

 One thing to note is that the RTAV feature only works with the PCoIP protocol and does not work with RDP.

Horizon View Clients

In this section, we are briefly going to touch on the Horizon View Client, as it is an important part of the solution and it's how you connect to your virtual desktop machine.

The Horizon View Client is where the transmitted pixels from your virtual desktop machines are received, decoded, and displayed. There are two distinct types of Horizon View Client, a software-based version that gets installed on the endpoint device and a hardware-based version that uses zero clients with the client running on the Teradici chip.

We will cover the View Client in more detail in *Chapter 8, Horizon View Clients*.

The Horizon View Standard Edition licensing

Horizon View Standard Edition is licensed on a per-concurrent user model and is available in 10 user packs or 100 user packs. The license also includes vSphere for Desktop (ESXi and vCenter Server), VMware Workstation, and ThinApp licenses.

Summary

In this chapter, we discussed the Horizon View architecture and the different components that make up the complete solution. We covered the key technologies, such as an in-depth look into how linked clones work for optimizing storage, and then introduced you to some of the features that contribute towards delivering a great end user experience, such as delivering high-end graphics, unified communications, profile management, and how the PCoIP protocol delivers the desktop to the end user.

Now that you understand these features and components, how they work, and how they fit into the overall solution, we will be taking a deeper look into how to design a Horizon View environment in the next chapter.

3
Designing and Building a Horizon View 6.0 Infrastructure

In this chapter, we will start by taking a closer look at the design process, walking you through the planning stages on how to approach a **virtual desktop infrastructure (VDI)** project. Having now explained the key components of a Horizon View deployment in the previous chapter, we will now look at the reference architecture and how we start to put together a design, building out the infrastructure for a production deployment.

Proving the technology – from PoC to production

In this section, we are going to discuss how to approach a VDI project. This is a key and very important piece of work that needs to be completed in the very early stages and is somewhat different from how you would typically approach an IT project.

Our starting point is to focus on the end users rather than the IT department. After all, these are the people that will be using the solution on a daily basis and know what tools they need to get their jobs done. Rather than giving them what you think they need, let's ask them what they actually need and then, within reason, deliver this. It's that old saying of don't try and fit a square peg into a round hole. No matter how hard you try, it's just never going to fit. First and foremost we need to design the technology around the user requirements rather than building a backend infrastructure only to find that it doesn't deliver what the users require.

Assessment

Once you have built your business case and validated that against your EUC strategy and there is a requirement for delivering a VDI solution, the next stage is to run an assessment. It's quite fitting that this book is entitled "Essentials", as this stage of the project is exactly that, and is essential for a successful outcome.

We need to build up a picture of what the current environment looks like, ranging from looking at what applications are being used to the type of access devices. This goes back to the earlier point about giving the users what they need and the only way to find that out is to conduct an assessment. By doing this, we are creating a baseline. Then, as we move into defining the success criteria and proving the technology, we have the baseline as a reference point to demonstrate how we have improved current working and delivered on the business case and strategy.

There are a number of tools that can be used in the assessment phase to gather the information required, for example, Liquidware Labs Stratusphere FIT or SysTrack from Lakeside Software.

Don't forget to actually talk to the users as well, so you are armed with the hard-and-fast facts from an assessment as well as the user's perspective.

Defining the success criteria

The key objective in defining the success criteria is to document what a "good" solution should look like for the project to succeed and become production-ready.

We need to clearly define the elements that need to function correctly in order to move from proof of concept to proof of technology, and then into a pilot phase before deploying into production. You need to fully document what these elements are and get the end users or other project stakeholders to sign up to them. It's almost like creating a statement of work with a clearly defined list of tasks.

Another important factor is to ensure that during this phase of the project, the criteria don't start to grow beyond the original scope. By that, we mean other additional things should not get added to the success criteria or at least not without discussion first. It may well transpire that something key was missed; however, if you have conducted your assessment thoroughly, this shouldn't happen.

Another thing that works well at this stage is to involve the end users. Set up a steering committee or advisory panel by selecting people from different departments to act as sponsors within their area of business. Actively involve them in the testing phases, but get them on board early as well to get their input in shaping the solution.

Too many projects fail when an end user tries something that didn't work. However, the thing that they tried is not actually a relevant use case or something that is used by the business as a critical line of business application and therefore shouldn't derail the project.

If we have a set of success criteria defined up front that the end users have signed up to, anything outside that criteria is not in scope. If it's not defined in the document, it should be disregarded as not being part of what success should look like.

Proving the technology

Once the previous steps have been discussed and documented, we should be able to build a picture around what's driving the project. We will understand what you are trying to achieve/deliver and, based upon hard-and-fast facts from the assessment phase, be able to work on what success should look like. From there, we can then move into testing some form of the technology should that be a requirement.

There are three key stages within the testing cycle to consider, and it might be the case that you don't need all of them. The three stages we are talking about are as follows:

- **Proof of concept** (PoC)
- **Proof of technology** (PoT)
- Pilot

In the next sections, we are briefly going to cover what each of these stages mean and why you might or might not need them.

Proof of concept

A proof of concept typically refers to a partial solution, typically built on any old hardware kicking about, that involves a relatively small number of users usually within the confines of the IT department acting in business roles, to establish whether the system satisfies some aspect of the purpose it was designed for.

Once proven, one or two things happen. Firstly nothing happens as it's just the IT department playing with technology and there wasn't a real business driver in the first place. This is usually down to the previous steps not having been defined. In a similar way, by not having any success criteria, it will also fail, as you don't know exactly what you are setting out to prove.

The second outcome is that the project moves into a pilot phase that we will discuss in a later section. You could consider moving directly into this phase and bypassing the PoC altogether. Maybe a demonstration of the technology would suffice, and using a demo environment over a longer period would show you how the technology works.

Proof of technology

In contrast to the PoC, the objective of a proof of technology is to determine whether or not the proposed solution or technology will integrate into your existing environment and therefore demonstrate compatibility. The objective is to highlight any technical problems specific to your environment, such as how your bespoke systems might integrate.

As with the PoC, a PoT is typically run by the IT department and no business users would be involved. A PoT is purely a technical validation exercise.

Pilot

A pilot refers to what is almost a small-scale roll out of the solution in a production-style environment that would target a limited scope of the intended final solution. The scope may be limited by the number of users who can access the pilot system, the business processes affected, or the business partners involved.

The purpose of a pilot is to test, often in a production-like environment, whether the system is working, as it was designed while limiting business exposure and risk. It will also touch *real* users so as to gauge the feedback from what would ultimately become a live, production solution. This is a critical step in achieving success, as the users are the ones that have to interact with the system on a daily basis, and the reason why you should set up some form of working group to gather their feedback.

That would also mitigate the project from failing, as the solution may deliver everything the IT department could ever wish for, but when it goes live and the first user logs on and reports a bad experience or performance, you may as well not be bothered.

The pilot should be carefully scoped, sized, and implemented. We will discuss this in the next section.

The pilot phase

In this section, we are going to discuss the pilot phase in a bit more detail and break it down into three distinct stages. These are important, as the output from the pilot will ultimately shape the design of your production environment.

The following diagram shows the workflow we will follow in defining our project:

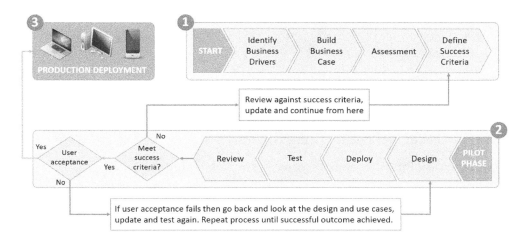

Phase 1 – pilot design

The pilot infrastructure should be designed on the same hardware platforms that the production solution is going to be deployed, for example, the same servers and storage. This takes into account any anomalies between platforms and configuration differences that could affect things such as scalability or more importantly performance.

Even at pilot stage, the design is absolutely key, and you should make sure you take into account the production design even at this stage. Why? Basically because many pilot solutions end up going straight into production and more and more users get added above and beyond those scoped for the pilot.

It's great going live with the solution and not having to go back and rebuild it, but when you start to scale by adding more users and applications, you might have some issues due to the pilot sizing. It may sound obvious, but often with a successful pilot, the users just keep on using it and additional users get added. If it's only ever going to be a pilot, that's fine, but keep this in mind and ask the question; if you are planning on taking the pilot straight into production design it for production.

It is always useful to work from a prerequisite document to understand the different elements that need consideration in the design. Key design elements include:

- Hardware sizing (servers – CPU, memory, and consolidation ratios)
- Pool design (based on user segmentation)
- Storage design (local SSD, SAN, and acceleration technologies)
- Image creation (rebuild from scratch and optimize for VDI)
- Network design (load balancing and external access)
- Antivirus considerations
- Application delivery (delivering virtually versus installing in core image)
- User profile management
- Floating or dedicated desktop assignments
- Persistent or non-persistent desktop builds (linked clone or full clone)

Once you have all this information, you can start to deploy the pilot.

Phase 2 – pilot deployment

In the deployment phase of the pilot, we are going to start building out the infrastructure, deploying the test users, building the OS images, and then start testing.

Phase 3 – pilot test

During the testing phase, the key thing during this stage is to work closely with the end users and your sponsors, showing them the solution and how it works, closely monitoring the users, and assessing the solution as it's being used. This allows you to keep in contact with the users and give them the opportunity to continually provide real-time feedback. This also allows you to answer questions and make adjustments and enhancements on the fly rather than wait to the end of the project and then to be told it didn't work or they just simply didn't understand something.

This then leads us onto the last section, the review.

Phase 4 – pilot review

This final stage sometimes tends to get forgotten. We have deployed the solution, the users have been testing it, and then it ends there for whatever reason. However, there is one very important last thing to do to enable the customer to move to production.

We need to measure the user experience or the IT department's experience against the success criteria we set out at the start of this process. We need to get customer sign off and agreement that we have successfully met all the objectives and requirements. If this is not the case, we need to understand the reasons why. Have we missed something in the use case, have the user requirements changed, or is it simply a perception issue?

Whatever the case, we need to cycle round the process again. Go back to the use case, understand and reevaluate the user requirements, (what it is that is seemingly failing or not behaving as expected), and then tweak the design or make the required changes and get them to test the solution again. We need to continue this process until we get acceptance and sign off; otherwise, we will not get to the final solution deployment phase.

When the project has been signed off after a successful pilot test, there is no reason why you cannot deploy the technology in production.

Now that we have talked about how to prove the technology and successfully demonstrated that it delivers against both our business case and user requirements, in the next sections, we are going to start looking at the design for our production environment.

Designing a Horizon 6.0 architecture

We are going to start this section by looking at the VMware reference architecture for Horizon View 6.0 before we go into more detail around the design considerations, best practice, and then sizing guidelines. In the final section, we will discuss some specific design examples.

The pod and block reference architecture

VMware has produced a reference architecture model for deploying Horizon View, with the approach being to make it easy to scale the environment by adding set component pieces of infrastructure, known as **View blocks**. To scale the number of users, you add View blocks up to the maximum configuration of five blocks. This maximum configuration of five View blocks is called a **View pod**.

The important numbers to remember are that each View block supports up to a maximum of 2,000 users, and a View pod is made up of up to five View blocks, therefore supporting a maximum of 10,000 users. The View block contains all the infrastructure required to host the virtual desktop machines, so appropriately sized ESXi hosts, a vCenter Server, and the associated networking and storage requirements. We will cover the sizing aspects later on in this chapter.

The following diagram shows an individual View block:

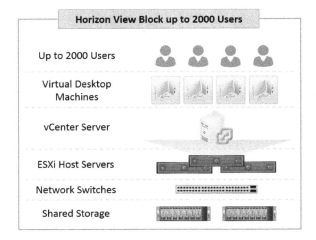

Apart from having a View block that supports the virtual desktop machines, there is also a management block for the supporting infrastructure components. The management block contains the management elements of Horizon View, such as the connection servers and security servers.

These will also be virtual machines hosted on the vSphere platform but using separate ESXi hosts and vCenter servers from those being used to host the desktops. The following diagram shows a typical View management block:

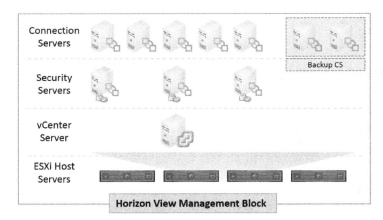

The management block contains the key Horizon View components to support the maximum configuration of 10,000 users or a View pod.

In terms of connection servers, the management block consists of a maximum of seven connection servers. This is often written as 5 + 2, which can be misleading, but what it means is you can have five connection servers and two that serve as backups to replace a failed server. Each connection server supports one of the five blocks, with the two spare in reserve in the event of a failure.

As we discussed previously, the View Security Servers are paired with one of the connection servers in order to provide external access to the users. In our example diagram, we have drawn three security servers meaning that these servers are configured for external access, while the others serve the internal users only.

In this scenario, the View Connection Servers and View Security Servers are deployed as virtual machines, and are therefore controlled and managed by vCenter. The vCenter Server can run on a virtual machine, or you can use the vCenter Virtual Appliance. It can also run on a physical Windows Server, as it's just a Windows application.

The entire infrastructure is hosted on a vSphere cluster that's separate from that being used to host the virtual desktop machines.

There are a couple of other components that are not shown in the diagram, and those are the databases required for View such as the events database and for View Composer.

If we now look at the entire Horizon View pod and block architecture for up to 10,000 users, the architecture design would look something like the following diagram:

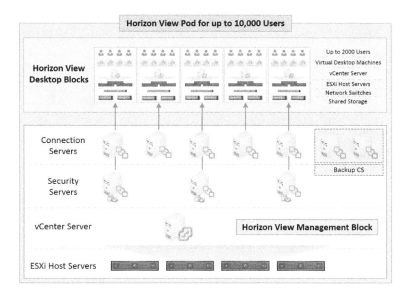

One thing to note is that although a pod is limited to 10,000 users, you can deploy more than one pod should you need an environment that exceeds the 10,000 users. Bear in mind though that the pods do not communicate with each other and will effectively be completely separate deployments.

As this is potentially a limitation in the scalability, but more so for disaster recovery purposes, where you need to have two pods across two sites for disaster recovery, there is a feature in Horizon View 6.0 that allows you to deploy pods across sites. This is called the **Cloud Pod Architecture (CPA)**, and we will cover this in the next section.

The Cloud Pod Architecture

The Cloud Pod Architecture, also referred to as **linked-mode View (LMV)** or **multidatacenter View (MDCV)**, allows you to link up to four View pods together across two sites, with a maximum number of supported users of up to 20,000.

There are four key features available by deploying Horizon View using this architecture:

- **Scalability**: This hosts more than 10,000 users on a single site
- **Multidatacenter support**: This supports View across more than one data center
- **Geo roaming**: This supports roaming desktops for users moving across sites
- **DR**: This delivers resilience in the event of a data center failure

Let's take a look at the Cloud Pod Architecture in the following diagram to explain the features and how it builds on the pod and block architecture we discussed previously:

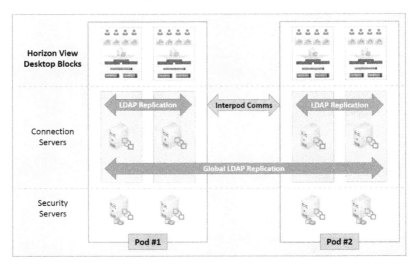

With the Cloud Pod Architecture, user information is replicated globally and the pods are linked using the **View interpod API (VIPA)** – the setup for which is command-line-based.

For scalability, with the Cloud Pod Architecture model, you have the ability to entitle users across pools on both different pods and sites. This means that, if you have already scaled beyond a single pod, you can link the pods together to allow you to go beyond the 10,000 user limit and also administer your users from a single location.

The pods can, apart from being located on the same site, also be on two different sites to deliver a mutlidatacenter configuration running as active/active. This also introduces DR capabilities. In the event of one of the data centers failing or losing connectivity, users will still be able to connect to a virtual desktop machine.

Users don't need to worry about what View Connection Server they need to use to connect to their virtual desktop machine. The Cloud Pod Architecture supports a single namespace with access via a global URL. As users can now connect from anywhere, there are some configuration options that you need to consider as to how they access their virtual desktop machine and from where it gets delivered. There are three options that form part of the **global user entitlement feature**:

- **Any**: This is delivered from any pod as part of the global entitlement
- **Site**: This is delivered from any pod from the same site the user is connecting from
- **Local**: This is delivered only from the local pod that the user is connected to

It's not just the users that get the global experience; the administrators can also be segregated in this way so that you can deliver delegated management.

Administration of pods could be delegated to the local IT teams on a per region/geo basis, with some operations such as provisioning and patching performed locally on the local pods or maybe it's so that local language support can be delivered. It is only global policy that is managed globally, typically from an organizations global HQ.

Now that we have covered some of the high-level architecture options, you should now be able to start to look at your overall design, factoring in locations and the number of users.

In the next section, we will start to look at how to size some of these components.

Sizing the infrastructure

In this section, we are going to discuss the sizing of the components previously described in the architecture section. We will start by looking at the management blocks containing the connection servers, security servers, and then the servers that host the desktops before finishing off with the desktops themselves.

The management block and the block hosting the virtual desktop machines should be run on separate infrastructure (ESXi hosts and vCenter Servers); the reason being due to the different workload patterns between servers and desktops and to avoid performance issues. It's also easier to manage, as you can determine what desktops are and what servers are, but more importantly it's also the way in which the products are licensed. With vSphere for desktop that comes with Horizon View, it only entitles you to run workloads that are hosting and managing the virtual desktop infrastructure.

Management servers

As we have discussed, the management servers run the infrastructure required to manage and administer the virtual desktop machines. In this section, we will look at the sizing recommendations for the management server roles, starting with the underlying infrastructure first.

ESXi host servers

The host servers for the management functions should be sized depending on the number of View Connection Servers, View Security Servers, and virtual desktop machines, the latter being the most important. If you are deploying infrastructure for a proof of concept, you can easily limit the amount of capacity required; however, this is where you need to consider whether or not you are planning on switching from the pilot straight into production. If that's the case, you need to size to the maximum of your environment so that you can scale up the infrastructure without issue. So, you would size your ESXi cluster so that it can host the maximum number of connection servers, security servers, and other components.

The View Connection Server

The View Connection Server is a Windows Server with View installed as an application. This Windows Server would be hosted as a virtual machine on the management block, and have a recommended configuration as shown in the following screenshot:

Horizon View Connection Server	
Supported operating systems	Windows Server 2008 R2
	Windows Server 2012 R2
Memory	10 GB
Virtual CPUs	4 vCPU
Hard disk space required	70 GB

As we have touched on previously, if this is purely for a PoC or pilot with a limited number of users, you can lower the specification to maybe two vCPUs and 4 GB of memory. You can't resize this afterwards; hence, you should size appropriately should you want to move straight into production without reinstalling.

The View replica server

The View replica server is essentially the same as the View Connection Server, as it acts as a backup to the main connection server. As such, it should be sized in exactly the same way as the connection server.

The View security server

As with the replica server, the security server is just another role of the connection server, meaning that it should be sized the same as these components.

The View Composer

The View Composer is slightly different from the connection server roles. It can either be installed on the same server as vCenter is running or as a standalone server.

The configuration recommendations for View Composer are detailed in the following screenshot:

Horizon View Composer	2,000 Users	10,000 Users
Supported operating systems	Windows Server 2008 R2 64-bit	Windows Server 2008 R2 64-bit
Memory	4 GB	10 GB
Virtual CPUs	2 vCPU	4 vCPU
Hard disk space required	40 GB	50 GB
Maximum desktop pool size	1,000	2,000

vCenter Servers

With the latest version of Horizon View, you have the ability to manage all 10,000 users with a single vCenter Server; however, that is probably not the best way of doing it, as you have no failover should your vCenter Server fail.

The configuration recommendation for vCenter Server is detailed in the following screenshot:

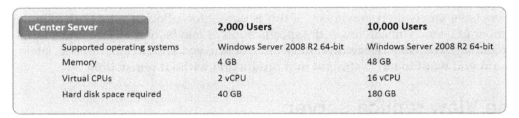

vCenter Server	2,000 Users	10,000 Users
Supported operating systems	Windows Server 2008 R2 64-bit	Windows Server 2008 R2 64-bit
Memory	4 GB	48 GB
Virtual CPUs	2 vCPU	16 vCPU
Hard disk space required	40 GB	180 GB

In the next section, we'll look at sizing the infrastructure to host the virtual desktops.

Sizing the desktop host servers

We will start this section by looking at core resources such as CPU, memory, networking, storage, and what to consider for hosting your virtual desktop machines in your View deployment.

In the final part of this section, we will look at some of the more high-end features such as sizing for hardware accelerated graphics.

CPU sizing considerations

One of the most asked questions when sizing the servers that are hosting the virtual desktop machines is how many can I fit on each host server, or how many virtual desktops per core? Well the answer is "it depends!."

Firstly, it depends on the CPU resources that your desktops are going to consume and the answer to that question will only come from your assessment data.

Secondly, and more obviously, it will depend on the CPU you configure in the host servers. This is usually chosen on price/performance, as there is usually a CPU that makes more financial sense and the best cost per desktop model.

For this section, as we don't have any actual assessment data to work from, we will use some assumptions on the types of users and CPU requirements for each type of user. We will base our calculations on an industry-standard, rack-mount server configured with two Intel Xeon E5-2690v2 CPUs that run at 3.0 GHz and have 10 cores per CPU, giving us a total of 20 cores per host server.

In the example calculations, you will also notice that we have subtracted two of the cores from the total available cores on the host server. The reason for this is that the hypervisor layer (ESXi) also needs CPU resource in order to run.

The following classifies the typical user profile and then gives an indication of the per-core ratio and how we arrived at that figure.

Light user

Typical utilization is around 300 MHz of CPU resource. It's also worth adding some additional resources to cover any peaks in workload and also other tasks such as sounds and USB devices. For this example, we will add 10 percent to the 300 MHz.

The profile of this user type would be somebody working in a call center, an administrator, or the basic web-browser-type user. These desktops might be suspended for long periods of time and have very low utilization, running just one or two light applications. We can work out the CPU requirements with the following quick calculation:

(CPU Speed in MHz x (Number of Cores – 2) ÷ CPU requirements of each virtual desktop

(3000 MHz x 18 Cores) ÷ 275 MHz = 196.36 desktops

In this user scenario, using our standard sever we described previously, we can host approximately 196 virtual desktop machines, giving us 11 users per core.

Medium user

Typical utilization is around 500 MHz of CPU resource plus 10 percent. This type of user would be something like data entry personnel, doctors, students, Microsoft Office users, or a help desk operator. These desktops will mainly be used during business/office hours and not heavily utilized. We can work out the CPU requirements with the following quick calculation:

(CPU Speed in MHz x (Number of Cores − 2) ÷ CPU requirements of each virtual desktop

(3000 MHz x 18 Cores) ÷ 550 MHz = 98.18 desktops

In this user scenario, using our standard sever we described previously, we can host approximately 98 virtual desktop machines, giving us six users per core.

Heavy user

Typical utilization is around 750 MHz of CPU resource plus 10 percent. This type of user would be something like a developer, system administrator, IT worker, database administrator, or engineer. These desktops will more than likely be heavily utilized throughout the day and also after normal business hours. They may also be running more graphically intensive or Java-based applications that increase the utilization of the desktop. We can work out the CPU requirements with the following quick calculation:

(CPU Speed in MHz x (Number of Cores − 2) ÷ CPU requirements of each virtual desktop

(3000 MHz x 18 Cores) ÷ 825 MHz = 65.45 desktops

In this user scenario, using our standard sever we described previously, we can host approximately 65 virtual desktop machines, giving us 4 users per core.

What we have highlighted in the previous user scenarios is based on assumptions and example use cases. This is where your assessment data becomes critical, as it will tell you the actual resource requirement figures for you own environment.

Memory sizing considerations

Sizing the memory for the servers hosting the virtual desktop machine is somewhat easier than the CPU, although you might need to play a balancing act with the chosen server. The reason is that, just because it can accommodate the number of desktops from a CPU perspective, it might not have the memory capacity to serve that number.

We will typically deploy Microsoft Windows 7 Professional, which will require approximately 2 GB of memory. If we took the light user scenario from the previous section, we would be hosting 196 virtual desktop machines. If each one is configured with 2 GB of memory, we will need 392 GB of memory just to host them and we will also need enough memory to run the hypervisor too.

Depending on your choice of server hardware, you might not be able to configure this amount of memory or it might be too expensive, in which case you might end up deploying more, but lower-configuration servers.

> One important thing when sizing and configuring memory for the virtual desktop machines is to *never over-commit the memory* and set the memory reservation to 100 percent. This stops the swap file from being created, saves storage capacity, and helps performance.

Networking considerations

The network optimization is key to giving the users a great experience, as this is how their virtual desktop machine is going to be delivered, and you need to consideration a couple of different factors when sizing the network.

Firstly, you need to look back at your different use cases, paying close attention to where the end users will be connecting from and whether they are LAN- or WAN-based. You also need to consider those that are remote and connect via the Internet, although there is nothing you can do from a network perspective for these users; however, you can configure polices that limit some of the features and capabilities that would consume more bandwidth.

On the subject of bandwidth, the question of how much bandwidth is required often pops up in conversation, and again it depends on what the users are doing that will determine how much they would consume. This is something that the assessment data will tell you; however, VMware has published some guideline figures as shown in the following screenshot:

Average Bandwidth Requirements	Typical Tasks	Average Bandwidth
Light user	Basic office productivity, no video or high-end graphics	50 - 150 Kbps
Medium user	Office productivity optimized for Horizon View	250 Kbps - 1 Mbps
Heavy user	Advanced office user with 3D graphics, Aero	400 Kbps - 2 Mbps
Power user	High-end user running video and CAD applications	2 Mbps +

The figures in the previous table refer to the bandwidth requirements overall, but depending on the bandwidth that's available, this will also dictate the audio bandwidth and ultimately the audio quality. This is outlined in the following screenshot:

Audio Bandwidth Requirements	Available Network Bandwidth	Audio Usage
CD quality audio	Up to 8 Mbps	1,500 Kbps
Stereo audio	Between 2 and 8 Mbps	400 Kbps
Mono audio	Between 700 Kbps and 2 Mbps	90 Kbps
Compressed mono audio	Between 125 Kbps and 700 Kbps	60 Kbps

It's worth noting that, if you cannot provide at least the minimum bandwidth requirements for audio, audio will be disabled for that particular session.

The PCoIP protocol is completely configurable using Windows group policy so that you can tune the user experience accordingly. We will cover more on how to tune and optimize the virtual desktop machines in *Chapter 9, Fine-tuning the End User Experience*.

There are two other considerations when looking at the networking aspects of your View deployment; the first is the latency of the connection.

We previously discussed bandwidth and what is required for the different use cases, but latency can also have a big impact on the end-user experience. Typically, the maximum tolerance is anything between 250 milliseconds and 300 milliseconds for acceptable performance. Anything above this may well work but could result in a degraded user experience; however, this would depend on the use case. For example, a basic office worker may work fine when compared with a heavy user. This is the information you would determine from your pilot with the end users.

Storage

When it comes to storage, we need to look at two aspects: performance and capacity. Back in *Chapter 2, Horizon View 6.0 Architectural and Feature Overview*, we discussed linked clones and how they reduce the storage capacity requirements by building each desktop as a snapshot that grows in time. The replica from which it originates needs to be located on fast storage, either local to the host server or via a SAN. To enable this in Horizon View, you are able to choose the location of where the replica should live, and one of the recommendations is that the replica sits on fast storage, such as local SSD, for example.

Alternative solutions would be to deploy some form of storage acceleration technology to drive the IOPS requirements. Horizon View also has its own integrated solution called the **View Storage Accelerator (VSA)** or **Content Based Read Cache (CBRC)**. This feature allows you to allocate up to 2 GB of memory from the underlying ESXi host server that can be used as a cache for the most commonly read blocks. As we are talking about booting up desktop operating systems, the same blocks are required, and as these can be retrieved from memory, the process is accelerated.

Another solution is the **View Composer Array Integration (VCAI)**, which allows the process of building linked clones to be offloaded to the storage array, and its native snapshot mechanism, rather than taking CPU cycles from the host server.

There are also a number of other third-party solutions that resolve the storage performance bottleneck, such as Atlantis Computing and their ILIO products, Nutanix, Nimble, and Tintri, to name a few others. So how many IOPS do you need?

As with the question on how many virtual desktop machines you can configure per core, the answer to the IOPS question is also "it depends!". If you read some of the guides and white papers on the subject, you will probably see something like Windows 7 needing 20 to 25 IOPS. That might be correct for steady state, but what about for peak disk activity? The only way you will know the answer to how many IOPS you need is from analyzing your assessment report data. While the desktop may well drive 25 IOPS, what about any applications running on that desktop? How many IOPS will the application require? You don't want to find out the answer to this after you have deployed your solution.

There is also the debate around the split of IOPS between read and write. It is often quoted that the split is 80:20 with 80 writes and 20 reads, but this again will be dependent on your environment and the actual answer will be in your assessment data. It may well transpire that you have 70:30 or even 60:40.

As the IOPS requirements are a key part to the sizing exercise and can have a hit on the virtual desktop machine performance, we need to get this right, so let's take a closer look at some actual sizing calculations.

One thing that gets forgotten when sizing is the RAID penalty or IOPS penalty when writing to the disks. This means that, for every read operation, there will be multiple write operations occurring depending on the RAID level being used.

For our example, we will work with RAID 5, which has a write penalty of 4, and we need to deliver 200 IOPS with a 60:40 read/write ratio. To calculate this, we can use the following formula:

> *(Total Workload IOPS * Percentage of read operations)*
> *+*
> *(Total Workload IOPS * Percentage of read operations) * RAID IO Penalty))*

Going back to our example, the calculation would look something like the following:

> *(200 IOPS * 60% read operations)*
> *+*   *= 600 IOPS*
> *(200 IOPS * 60% read operations) * 4))*

So in this example, we would need to configure a RAID 5 array that could deliver the 600 IOPS that we require.

Delivering high-end graphics

In *Chapter 2, Horizon View 6.0 Architectural and Feature Overview*, we discussed the two options to delivering high-end graphics from a virtual desktop machine. In the next sections, we are going to look at the configuration options and design considerations for deploying hardware-based graphics in Horizon View with vSGA and vDGA.

Virtual shared graphics acceleration considerations

In this section, we will look at the things you need to think about if you are going to deploy the shared graphics model.

vSGA Supported Configurations

vSGA will support OpenGL 2.1- and DirectX 9-based applications running on Windows 7 and eight virtual desktop machines, virtualized on the VMware vSphere 5.1 platform and above, and using one of the following supported NVIDIA GPU cards:

- Quadro 4000, 5000, and 6000

- Tesla M2070-Q
- Grid K1 and K2

There is also a hardware compatibility list that details which servers support these graphics cards (http://tinyurl.com/msdzu6b).

How many virtual desktops are supported with vSGA?

This is a question that gets asked most often when talking about delivering hardware-based graphics within a Horizon View environment, so let's spend some time explaining some of this in this section. Within Horizon View, you would create different desktop pools depending on the use case, as we will cover in *Chapter 8, Horizon View Clients*. One of the desktop pools would be configured to use high-end graphics, as typically you would not give all users access to a hardware-based GPU.

So to answer the question, the number of virtual desktops you can allocate to a GPU is dependent on the amount of video memory (VRAM) that you allocate to each virtual desktop. The thing to bear in mind is that the resources are shared and therefore normal VMware virtualization rules apply. The first thing to note is how memory is shared.

 Half of the video memory allocated to a virtual desktop machine is allocated from the GPU card's memory, and the other half is from the host server's memory. When sizing your host servers, you need to ensure that you have enough memory configured in the server to allocate this as video memory.

Based on that, and the number of virtual desktops supported being based on the amount of allocated VRAM, let's looks at how that works out. So, the default amount of VRAM allocated to a virtual desktop machine is 128 MB. So, in this example, 64 MB will come from the GPU and the other 64 MB from the host server. If you then take a GPU card that has 4 GB of VRAM onboard, you will be able to support 64 virtual desktops (*4 GB or 4096 MB divided by 64 MB from the GPU is equal to 64 virtual desktop machines*).

Within Horizon View, you can allocate a maximum of 512 MB of VRAM per virtual desktop machine. If you apply this to the previous example using the same 4 GB GPU card, you now reduce the number of supported virtual desktops down to 16 (*4 GB or 4,096 MB divided by 256 MB from the GPU is equal to 16 virtual desktop machines*).

One thing to remember: if you cannot fulfill a virtual desktop machine's specification and there are insufficient resources, it won't boot or power on. This is the same for the GPU configuration. If you configure a desktop pool with more virtual desktop machines than you can support on that GPU, these will not boot.

> If you do happen to configure more virtual desktop machines in a pool where you may not be able to guarantee the GPU resources to be available, set the **Hardware 3D** setting in the View Administrator console to **Automatic**. Doing this allows Horizon View to revert to software-based 3D rendering in order to deliver the virtual desktop machines.

Virtual dedicated graphics acceleration considerations

In this section, we will look at the things you need to think about if you are going to deploy the dedicated graphics model.

vDGA supported configurations

The following GPU cards are supported with vDGA:

- Quadro 2000, 4000, 5000, and 6000
- Quadro 1000M and 3000M
- Tesla M2070-Q
- GRID K1 and K2

How many virtual desktops are supported with vDGA?

Unlike the vSGA model that is limited by the amount of memory on the GPU card, vDGA is limited by the number of GPUs you can physically fit into the host server.

For example, an NVIDIA GRID K1 GPU card has four GPUs onboard, which would mean that you can allocate four virtual desktop machines to this card. Depending on your server hardware platform, you can install more than one card, therefore increasing the number of users that have access to a hardware-enabled GPU in their virtual desktop.

Sizing the virtual desktop machines

There are a couple of things to consider when we talk about designing and sizing the actual virtual desktop machines. Both are based on the use case of the end user and will also influence the pool design.

The first is the actual specification and functionality of the virtual desktop machine. For example, different departments might have varying requirements where perhaps a marketing or engineering department may need virtual desktop machines that are configured with high-end hardware accelerated graphics. You wouldn't want to give everyone this level of resource due to the infrastructure costs. So, in this example, you may have a graphics-enabled pool with access to an NVIDIA GPU.

The second concerns the user assignment to the desktop and whether they have their own dedicated desktop that they effectively own, or whether they are allocated a floating, stateless virtual desktop machine from a pool of preconfigured resources.

Pool design

You are going to want to design your desktop pools based upon the similarities between the desktops that will allow you to group virtual desktop machines together. We are going to utilize the information collected by the desktop assessment and other sources to start designing how your pools are going to look.

When analyzing this data, you are going to look for similarities between the applications and use cases and make decisions based on the information on how you will design these pools. As a best practice, you would look wherever possible to have the smallest number of desktop pools possible to ease the management of the environment, but you are also not going to want to take this to the nth degree, as trying to recompose ridiculously large pools can be difficult and time-consuming, and may have a performance impact. You may want to create a pool for different departments or maybe for different job functions. As you can see, this is going to be a very careful balancing act to get the pool design correct.

User assignments – dedicated or floating desktops?

We have already touched on whether or not a user should have a dedicated desktop or be allocated one from a pool, but in this section we are going to discuss the different types of desktop assignments we can deploy with Horizon View in a bit more detail.

One of the questions that always gets asked concerns having a dedicated or floating desktop assignment. Desktops can either be individual virtual machines that are dedicated to a user on a 1:1 basis, as we have in the physical world where the user owns their desktop, or the user will be assigned a new, Vanilla desktop that gets provisioned and personalized at the time of login, and can be chosen at random from a pool of available desktops that the user is entitled to. If you remember back to *Chapter 1, Introducing VDI and VMware Horizon 6.0*, we talked about building the composite desktop. The two assignment options are as follows:

- **Dedicated-assignment desktop**: A user is allocated a desktop that retains all of their documents, applications, and settings between sessions. The desktop is statically assigned the first time that the user connects, and is then used for all subsequent sessions. No other user is permitted access to the desktop.

- **Floating-assignment desktop**: A user might be connected to different desktops from within the pool each time they connect. User data does not persist between sessions and is delivered to the assigned virtual desktop machine as the user logs on. The desktop is refreshed or reset when the user logs off and reverts back to its Vanilla state. This is also referred to as a stateless desktop model.

In most use cases, a floating desktop configuration is the preferred option. The key reason is that, in this model, you don't need to build all the desktops up front for each user. You only need to power on a virtual desktop as and when it's required. All users start with the same basic desktop that then gets personalized before delivery. This helps with concurrency rates. For example, you may have 5,000 people in your organization but only 2,000 actually log in at the same time. Therefore, you will only need to have 2,000 virtual desktops available. Otherwise, you will have to build a desktop for every one of the 5,000 users that might ever log in, meaning more infrastructure and cost.

One thing to highlight is that there is often some confusion over dedicated and floating virtual desktop machine assignment and linked clones. Just to make it clear, linked clones and full clones are not what we are talking about when we refer to desktop assignment and whether the virtual desktop machine is dedicated or stateless. The cloning operations refer to how a desktop is built whereas the terms *dedicated* and *floating* refer to how a desktop is assigned to a user.

Dedicated and floating are purely about the user assignment and whether they are assigned a dedicated desktop or a stateless desktop. As we have already covered, linked clones are a feature of View Composer. That means that, regardless of having a floating or dedicated desktop assignment, the virtual desktop machine can still be a linked or full clone.

The final point is to look at your concurrency rate, as that has a bearing on the number of virtual desktop machines you need to have available and also how much infrastructure you need to host them.

Choosing the right client device

The subject of choosing the end user's client device often gets overlooked, but if you are looking to replace an existing PC estate with thin or zero clients, there are a few things that you need to be aware of when selecting the appropriate device.

The client device should reflect the use case for the users. While a zero client is an attractive option due to the lower management overheads, this type of device is hardware-based and therefore may not be able to support some of the features and functionality that the user requires. For example, some of the multimedia functions and unified communications solutions require specific elements that are only present in a full operating system. Codecs are a good example of this.

An example design exercise

In this section, we are going to put together all the parts we have covered in this chapter and build an example design based on a fictitious company called PVO Engineering Inc. and their requirements for deploying a VDI solution. This is shown in the following topology diagram of their current network environment and locations:

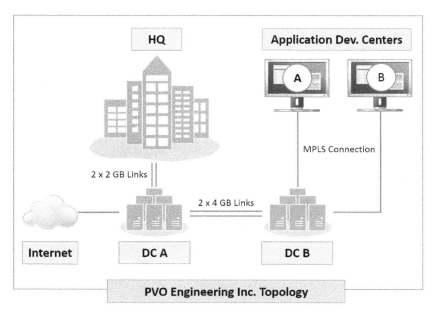

The company has three locations: an HQ office and two remote sites for the application development teams. To serve these, they have two data centers that are running active/active. Data center A supports the mobile and HQ workers, while data center B supports the application development teams. Each data center can support the entire environment in the event of a data center failure.

User requirements

We have conducted an assessment to gather information on the current user install base of 5,750 users, and we have built a picture of the types of users and their requirements, along with their location. This is detailed in the following screenshot:

User Types/Requirements	Qty	Location	What do they do / need?
Application Developers	125	Application development site A	Local admin rights to install software
	125	Application development site B	Local admin rights to install software
Office workers	2,000	HQ	Standard office applications
	1,500	HQ	Standard office + Project + Visio
Contractors	250	HQ	BYOD, require local admin rights
Engineering	150	HQ	Require CAD - high-end graphics
	100	HQ	Require 3D and video
Sales	1,500	Remote	Secure remote access

Now that we have the user requirements, we can start to look at creating a pool design based on these use cases.

The pool design

The pool design reflects the use cases and any similar desktops will be included into a single pool. Based on the information we have gathered, we can start building the pool design, which will start to look like the following:

Desktop Pools	DC	Pod	Pool Description	Number of Desktops
Application Developers	B	2	Dedicated global pool	250 (125 for each application dev. Center)
Office workers & Sales	A	1	Floating pool	5,000
Engineering - CAD	A	1	Dedicated pool with GPU	150
Engineering - Video	A	1	Dedicated pool with 3D	100
Contractors	A	1	Dedicated pool	250

All the office workers in the design are part of the same desktop pool, along with sales even though they have different application requirements. We will look at delivering these applications outside of the core virtual desktop machine image using ThinApp or the application publishing feature in Horizon View 6.

Using the pod and block architecture, we are going to deploy two View pods, one in datacenter A and the other in datacenter B. The reason being is that it makes more sense from the network perspective to have these desktops nearer to the users; however, we will take advantage of the Cloud Pod Architecture, as the developers travel between sites, and will configure a global pool for these users.

Now that we have an idea of the pools, we can start to shape the pod design and size the management blocks and the desktop hosting blocks. Let's start with the desktop blocks.

Sizing the desktop blocks

In data center A with pod 1, we have 5,500 virtual desktop machines. As there are 2,000 virtual desktop machines supported per block, we would need to configure three blocks with approximately 1,800 virtual desktop machines per block.

In datacenter B, we have 250 virtual desktop machines and so we only need one block.

The next question is how many servers do we need to host the virtual desktop machines? For this example, we will use the users-per-core figures previously discussed in this chapter to cover light users for the office and sales workers, and very heavy users for the developers and engineering users. That means that, for office users, we can configure 98 virtual desktop machines per host and, for the very heavy users, we can configure 50 virtual desktop machines per host.

We also need to remember that we have some distinct differences in the host server requirements, as the engineering users require access to hardware-based GPU. This would result in deploying a cluster for each. The number of hosts required for **Pod 1** would look something like the following:

Pod 1	No. of Users	Desktops per Server	No. of Hosts Required	Cluster
Office & Sales	5,000	98	52 + 1 for DR	A
Contractors	250	50	5 + 1 for DR	A
GPU - based CAD	150	8	19	B
GPU - based Video	100	60	2	B
Application Developers	250	50	5 + 1 for DR	A
		TOTAL	**86**	

For the GPU-based virtual desktop machines, we have configured two options. For CAD, we have used vDGA and for video, we have configured vSGA.

With vDGA, we have configured each host server with two NVidia GRID K2 cards, resulting in each host having the ability to host up to eight virtual desktop machines.

Pod 2 in datacenter B contains just the virtual desktop machines for the application development users and would look something like the following:

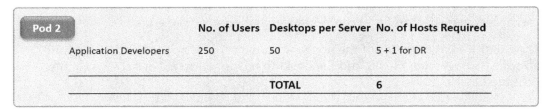

Pod 2	No. of Users	Desktops per Server	No. of Hosts Required
Application Developers	250	50	5 + 1 for DR
	TOTAL		6

With pod 1, we have exceeded the number of hosts we can support in a cluster, the limit being 32. Therefore, we would deploy two clusters per desktop block with the number of host servers divided across the clusters.

Sizing the storage requirements

Using the calculations we used previously, we can work out the IOPS requirements we need to deliver. We will base the calculation on a requirement of 30 IOPS per virtual desktop machine, a 30/70 read/write ratio, a RAID 5 array, and a 10 GB disk capacity.

Given those variables, we can work out what the storage requirements are, as shown in the following table:

Storage Requirements	No. of Users	IOPS Required	Capacity
Pod 1	5,500	412,500	55 TB
Pod 2	250	18,750	2.5 TB

Sizing the management blocks

Once we have configured the desktop blocks and know our pool configuration, we can look at sizing the management blocks to provide the supporting infrastructure.

We will configure the infrastructure components as follows:

View Component	Quantity in Pod 1	Quantity in Pod 2
Connection Server	6 (2 per block)	2 (2 per block)
Security Server	2 (external access)	0 (no external access required)
View Composer	3 (1 per block)	1 (1 per block)
vCenter Server	3 (1 per block)	1 (1 per block)

The final element to look at is the network. You need to assess whether or not the current network configuration will support the users. If not, then you may need to look at some form of network upgrade.

The network requirements

Now that we have our pool design, management and desktop blocks, and the storage requirements, we can look at the network requirements, as shown in the following screenshot:

Network Requirements	Pod No.	No. of Desktops	Bandwidth per Desktop	Total
Office & Sales	1	5,500	150 Kbps	825 Mbps
GPU-based users	1	250	500 Kbps	125 Mbps
Application Developers	2	250	500 Kbps	125 Mbps

Summary

In this chapter, we have covered some of the essential tasks in designing and building out our Horizon View infrastructure.

We started at a high-level discussing the approach to a VDI project and the different phases in which to work through in order to plan and test an environment. The most important of these phases is the assessment phase.

Once we had worked through these, we looked at the pod and block reference architecture before examining the sizing of the key Horizon View components, such as the connection server, security server, and View Composer.

Following on from the management architecture, we looked at some of the considerations for sizing and configuring the virtual desktop machines and the user assignments before finally putting this all together in a high-level example design.

You should now have a methodology for approaching a project coupled with the knowledge to be able to start sizing your environment specific to your end-user requirements.

In the next chapter, we will discuss how to install all the components that make up the Horizon View solution. We will have a deep dive into installation and follow the process using step-by-step screenshots; thus, by the end of the chapter, we will have a fully functional View infrastructure up and running.

Installing Horizon View 6.0

In this chapter, we are going to concentrate on getting Horizon View installed and running in our environment. Before we perform the install, we will cover some of the prerequisites and minimum requirements as well as what to download.

Preparing for the installation

Before starting the actual installation of any software components, we are first going to look at a few things you need to do in order to prepare your environment.

Welcome to our lab environment

Throughout the practical stages of this book, you have the opportunity to follow the tasks and steps that are being described using our example lab environment. Or, if you prefer, you can use the guides to set up your own environment, whether that's for a proof of concept, pilot, or production deployment.

What you need for the example lab

The example lab consists of the following infrastructure components and configuration:

- 2 x ESXi host servers running vSphere 5.5 U1

- 6 x Windows Server 2008 R2 SP1 Enterprise Edition virtual machines for the following roles, which we will configure throughout this chapter (you can also use Windows Server 2012):

    ° Domain controller for `pvolab.com` (hostname: `hzn6-dc`)

    ° Connection server (hostname: `hzn6-cs1`)

    ° Security server (hostname: `hzn6-ss1`)

- Replica server (hostname: `hzn6-cs2`)
- View Composer (hostname: `hzn6-composer`)
- 2 x SQL Express databases [one for View Composer and one for the events database (`hzn6-sql`)]

- 2 x Windows 7 virtual desktop machines
- 2 x Windows 8.1 virtual desktop machines
- 2 x vCenter Server Appliances or Windows-based vCenter Servers

All machines should be domain-joined with the exception of the security server. The environment looks something like the following diagram:

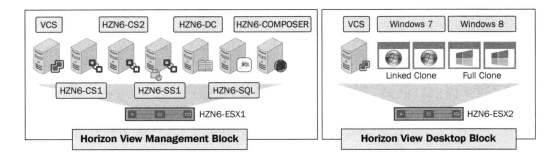

The Windows 7 and 8 virtual desktop machines are those that will be used to build our gold image or Parent Image and will become the replica when we start to deploy virtual desktop machines using View Composer.

Downloading the software

To download the software, first, log on to your **My VMware** portal using the `https://my.vmware.com/web/vmware/login` URL.

Click on the **All Products** tab, scroll down to **Desktop & End-User Computing** and the on **VMware Horizon (with View)** section (**1**). Click on **View Download Components** (**2**), as shown in the following screenshot:

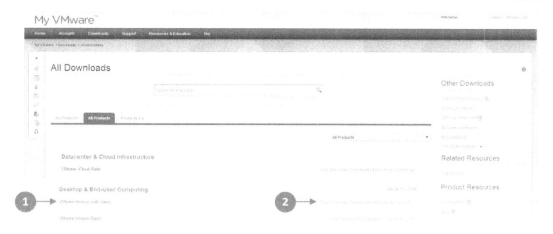

You will now see the different Horizon 6.0 editions listed.

We will download **Horizon View Standard Edition** and **VMware Horizon 6.0 (with View)**, as shown in the following screenshot:

Click on **Go to Downloads** (**3**) to view the software components (as shown in the preceding screenshot). From here, you can download the following software components:

- **Horizon View Connection Server (64-bit)**
- **Horizon View Agent (32-bit & 64-bit)**
- **Horizon Persona Management (32-bit & 64-bit)**
- **Horizon View Composer**
- **Horizon View Agent Direct-Connection (32-bit & 64-bit)**
- **Horizon View GPO Bundle**

For our example lab, we will download these installation files into a shared folder on our domain controller, which is also acting as our file server.

SSL certificates for Horizon View

From View 5.1 onwards, VMware introduced the use of certificates for the Horizon View components, which means that the connection server, security server, and so on need to have a certificate installed.

For this book, we are going to assume that for a production environment, you already have either a certificate of authority installed or are using a third-party certificate. However, if you are running a proof of concept or pilot in isolation from your production infrastructure, then in the next few sections, we will briefly cover how to set up certificates.

It is recommended that you already have a certificate installed on the server that will be used as your connection server prior to installing the connection server software and also have a Public CA for the security server.

Setting up a Root CA server

In this section, we are going to walk through the steps to set up a server that will act as our Root CA. For our example lab, we are going to use the domain controller for this role.

Adding the Root CA role

On the domain controller **HZN6-DC**, launch **Server Manager** and perform the following steps:

1. Click on **Roles** (**1**), and then click on **Add Roles** (**2**), as shown in the following screenshot:

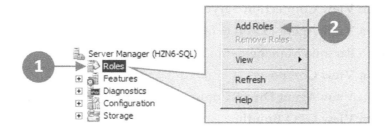

2. You will now see the **Before You Begin** page. Click on **Next >**.

3. In the **Roles** box, check the box for **Active Directory Certificate Services (3)**, and click on **Next >**.

4. On the **Introduction to Active Directory Certificate Services** page, click on **Next >**.

5. On the **Select Role Services** page shown in the following screenshot, check the box for **Certification Authority (4)**, and click on **Next >**:

6. On the **Specify Setup Type** page, click on the button for **Enterprise (5)**, and click on **Next >**:

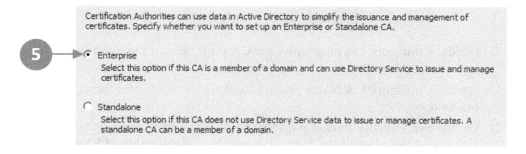

7. On the **Specify CA Type** page, click on the button for **Root CA (6)**, and click on **Next >**:

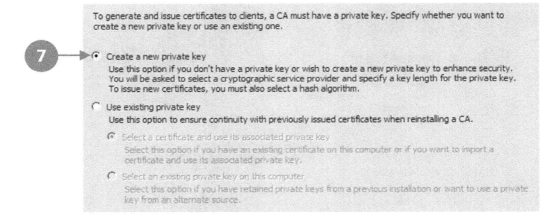

A combination of root and subordinate CAs can be configured to create a hierarchical public key infrastructure (PKI). A root CA is a CA that issues its own self-signed certificate. A subordinate CA receives its certificate from another CA. Specify whether you want to set up a root or subordinate CA.

6

(•) Root CA
   Select this option if you are installing the first or only certification authority in a public key infrastructure.

( ) Subordinate CA
   Select this option if your CA will obtain its CA certificate from another CA higher in a public key infrastructure.

8. On the **Set Up Private Key** page, click on the button for **Create a new private key (7)**, and click on **Next >**:

7

To generate and issue certificates to clients, a CA must have a private key. Specify whether you want to create a new private key or use an existing one.

(•) Create a new private key
   Use this option if you don't have a private key or wish to create a new private key to enhance security. You will be asked to select a cryptographic service provider and specify a key length for the private key. To issue new certificates, you must also select a hash algorithm.

( ) Use existing private key
   Use this option to ensure continuity with previously issued certificates when reinstalling a CA.

   (•) Select a certificate and use its associated private key
      Select this option if you have an existing certificate on this computer or if you want to import a certificate and use its associated private key.

   ( ) Select an existing private key on this computer
      Select this option if you have retained private keys from a previous installation or want to use a private key from an alternate source.

9. On the **Configure Cryptography for CA** page, accept the defaults, and click on **Next >**.

10. On the **Configure CA Name** page, accept the defaults, and then click on **Next >**.

11. On the **Set Validity Period** page, set a time for which certificates from this Root CA are valid for. We will leave the default value of **5 Years (8)**. Click on **Next >**:

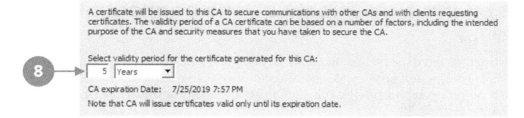

12. On the **Configure Certificate Database** page, accept the defaults and click on **Next >**.

13. On the **Confirm Installation Selections** page, ensure that you have entered your details correctly, and then click on **Install**.

14. You will now see that the installation was successful. The yellow colored warning is just saying that this server does not have the Windows automatic updating feature enabled:

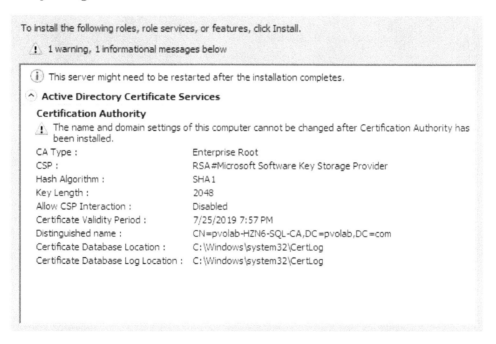

Now that we have everything in place, we can start the installation of the Horizon View software components, starting with installing the certificate on the connection server.

Installing a certificate on the connection server

Now that we have the certificate server in place, the next task is to install the certificate on the server prior to installing the View Connection Server software on the servers that will run the connection server roles. For this, perform the following steps:

1. In the server where you want to install the certificate, click on **Start**, and then click on **Run....** In the **Run** dialog box, type mmc (**1**) to open the Microsoft Management Console. In our example, we will use the server that will become our first connection server, which is **HZN6-CS1**, as shown in the following screenshot:

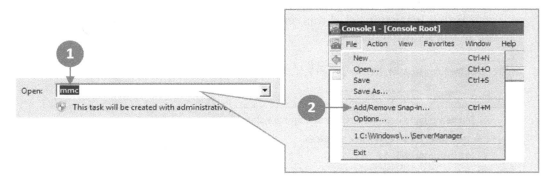

2. Now, click on **Add/Remove Snap-in...** (**2**) (shown in the preceding screenshot).
3. Click on **Certificates** (**3**) from the **Available snap-ins** list, and then click on **Add >** (**4**):

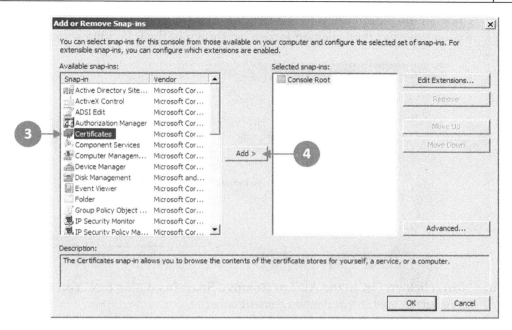

4. In the following **Certificates snap-in** dialog box, click on the button for **Computer account** (5), and click on **Next >**:

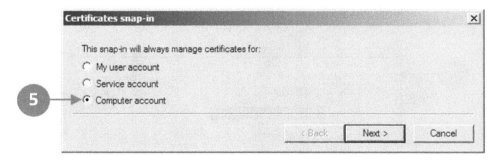

5. Click on the radio button for **Local computer** (6) from the **Select Computer** dialog box, and then click on **Finish**, as shown in the following screenshot:

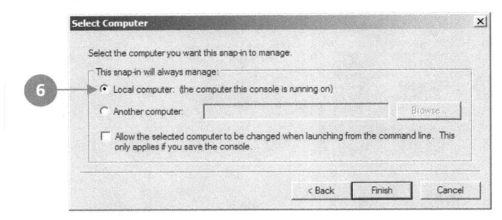

6. Now, click on **OK** in the **Add or Remove Snap-ins** dialog box. You will now have certificates in your management console.

7. Expand **Certificates (Local Computer)** (7), and then right-click on **Personal** (8). From the menu, click on **All Tasks** (9), and then select **Request New Certificate...** (10):

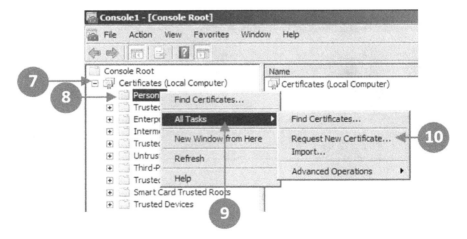

8. Click on **Next** to start the enrollment process, as shown in the following screenshot:

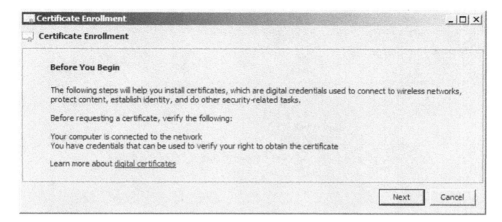

9. In the **Certificate Enrollment** dialog box, click on **Active Directory Enrollment Policy** (**11**), and then click on **Next**:

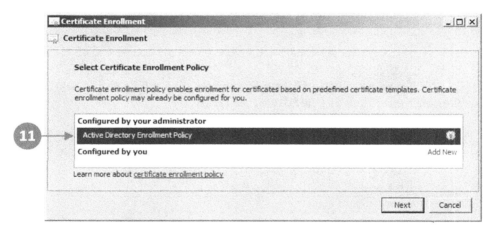

10. In the **Request Certificates** dialog box, check the box for **Computer** (12). We are going to use this policy template for our certificate. Now, click on the arrow next to **Details** (13), and then click on **Properties** (14):

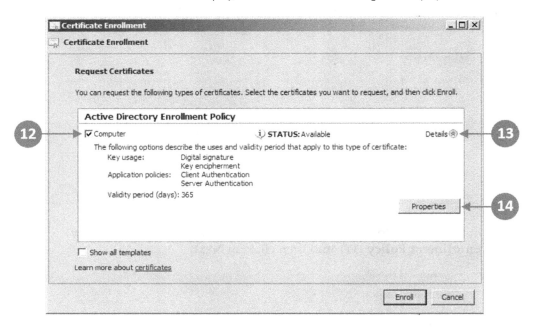

11. You will now see the **Certificate Properties** dialog box. In the first tab, **General**, enter vdm as **Friendly name** (16):

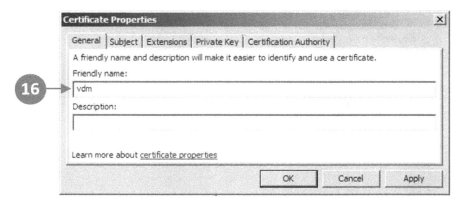

12. Now, click on the **Private Key** tab (17), and then expand the **Key options** section by clicking on the arrow next to it (18). Check the box for **Make private key exportable** (19):

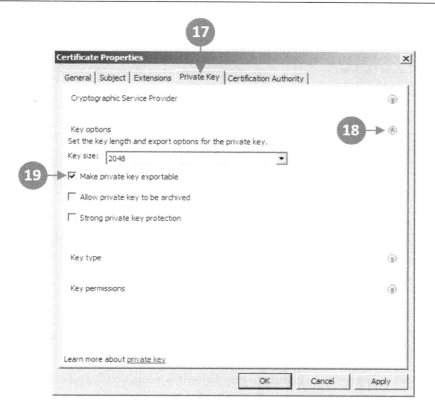

13. Next, click on the **Certification Authority** tab (**20**) and ensure that you check the box next to the appropriate certificate server. In our example, this is **pvolab-HZN6-DC-CA** (**21**):

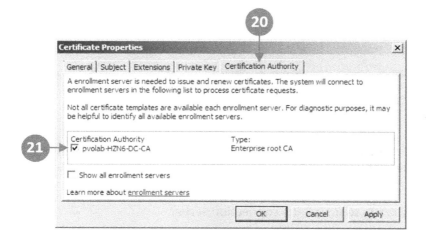

14. The configuration is now complete, so click on **Enroll** (**22**):

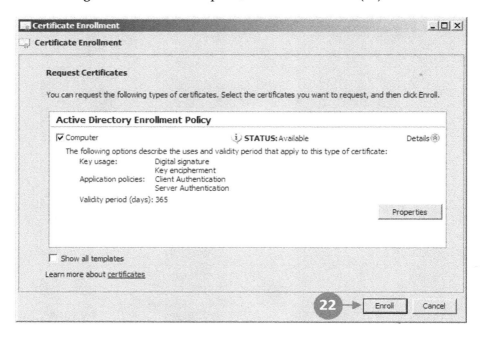

15. Check whether the certificate enrollment is successful, and click on **Finish**:

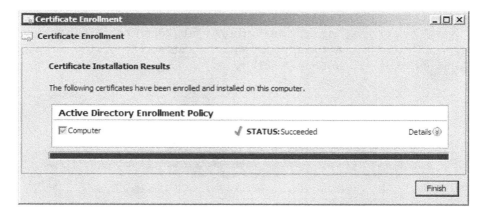

You will need a valid certificate on all the Horizon View server components, so you need to do this on security servers, replica servers, and so on in order to deploy it via a policy.

We are now ready to install the connection server.

Installing the Horizon View Connection Server

Now that we have set up Active Directory for our virtual desktop machines, we can start to install the Horizon View software components. We will start with the connection server.

 Don't forget to use the FQDN of the View Connection Server when you log in, as this is the entry in the SSL certificate. The icon on the desktop uses the localhost as its URL, which is not in the certificate name by default.

The minimum requirements of a connection server

Before we start with the installation, let's quickly cover the minimum specification requirements for the connection server. These are detailed in the following tables and cover hardware and operating system requirements

Hardware requirements

The following screenshot outlines the hardware requirements for the View Connection Server:

Server Requirements	Minimum Requirements	Recommended Config
Processor	Pentium IV running at 2.0 GHz	4 CPUs
Network	10/100 Mbps network card	1 Gbps network card
Memory	4 GB	10 GB

Software requirements – supported operating systems

The View Connection Server must be installed on one of the following supported Windows Server operating systems:

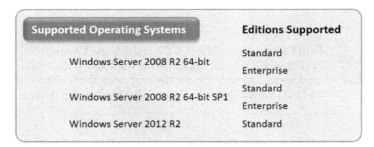

Supported Operating Systems	Editions Supported
Windows Server 2008 R2 64-bit	Standard
	Enterprise
Windows Server 2008 R2 64-bit SP1	Standard
	Enterprise
Windows Server 2012 R2	Standard

We now understand the prerequisites, so we will start the Horizon View installation, which we will cover in the next section.

 These hardware and software requirements also apply to the View security server and the View replica server.

The installation process

On the server that you are going to use as the connection server, locate the installation software you downloaded previously into the shared network folder, and launch the `VMware-viewconnectionserver-x86_64-6.0.0-1884746` installation file.

Note that the number at the end of the filename is the build number, and it might be different depending on the build or version of Horizon View you are installing.

The installation application is launched, as shown in the following screenshot:

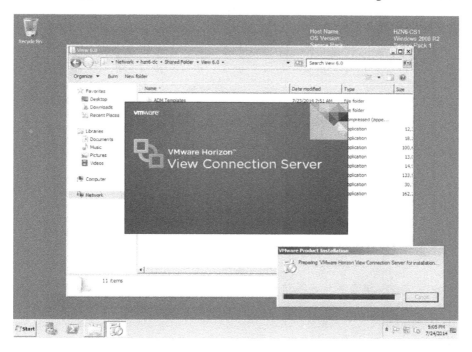

The steps to install Horizon View are as follows:

1. To start the installation, click on **Next >**, as shown in the following screenshot:

2. In the **License Agreement** dialog box, accept the license agreement by clicking on the button for **I accept the terms in the license agreement (1)**, and click on **Next >**:

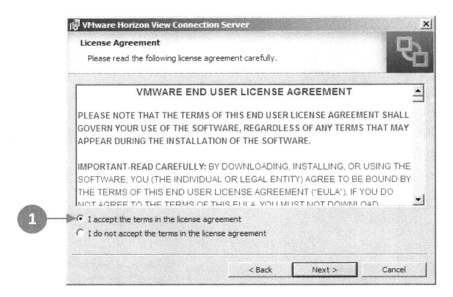

3. In the **Destination Folder** dialog box, click on **Change… (2)** to change the installation folder or click on **Next >** to accept the default location. In our example, we are going to stick with the default. Click on **Next >** to continue:

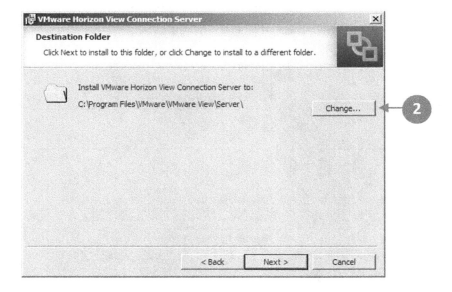

4. The next dialog box is **Installation Options**, where we choose which type of connection server we want to install. As we have discussed previously, the replica server and the security server are all different types of connection server roles. As this is the first connection server, we are going to select **View Standard Server (3)**.

5. We also want to allow our users to have access to their virtual desktop machines from an HTML5 browser, so we need to tick the **Install HTML Access (4)** box. In previous versions of View, the HTML access feature was installed as an add-on feature pack. It's now integrated into the overall installation process:

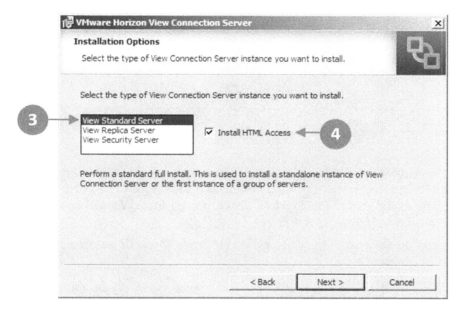

6. Click on **Next >** to continue.

7. Enter a password to protect the View Connection Server data (**5**) and re-enter it again (**6**). You can optionally set a password reminder (**7**). Click on **Next >** to continue:

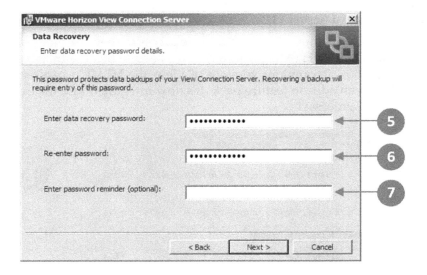

8. The **Firewall Configuration** dialog box allows you to automatically configure the Windows firewall ports that Horizon View requires in order to allow users to connect to their virtual desktop machines. We will detail the ports required in *Appendix*, *References*.

9. Click on the button for **Configure Windows Firewall automatically** (**8**), and click on **Next >**:

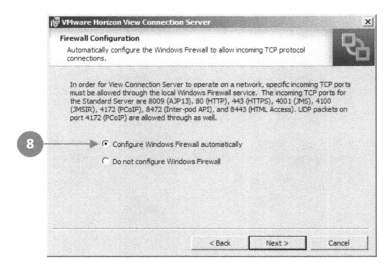

10. In the **Initial View Administrators** dialog box, we are going to select the users or groups who will become View administrators.

11. You can either choose to authorize all users in the local admins group or a domain user or group. In our example, we are going to click on the button for **Authorize a specific domain user or domain group** (9) and authorize the administrator account for our domain:

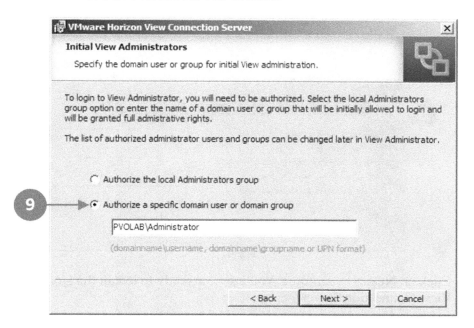

12. Click on **Next >** to continue.

13. The **User Experience Improvement Program** dialog box is optional and is used to collect usage stats for VMware. In our example, make sure that the **Participate anonymously in the user experience improvement program** box (**10**) is not ticked:

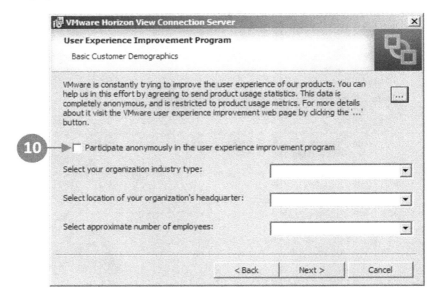

14. Click on **Next >** to continue. You are now ready to install the Horizon View Connection Server.

15. Click on **Install** to start to start the installation process:

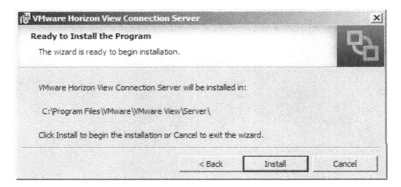

16. Finally, if you want to read the `readme` file, then check the box (**11**); otherwise, click on **Finish** to complete the installation process and close the installation application:

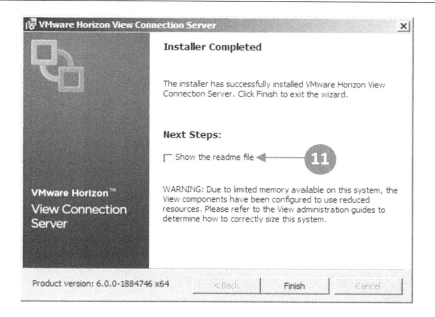

You have now installed your first instance of the Horizon View Connection Server, and you will see the shortcut icon on the desktop.

To ensure that the connection server is up and running, let's quickly log in using the following procedure. Before we do that, we need to ensure that you have Adobe Flash Player 10.1 or higher installed:

1. To log on to the connection server, type `https://<FQDN of connection server/admin`. So, for our example lab, this would look like `https://hzn6-cs1.pvolab.com/admin`.

2. You will now see the login page.

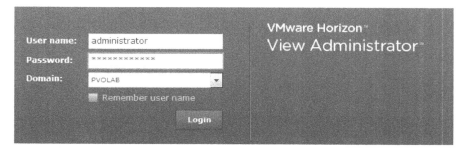

3. Log in using the administrator account and password, but before clicking on the **Login** button, let's quickly make sure that a certificate is installed.

4. For this, check the address bar in your browser and make sure there are no certificate errors and also look at the installed certificate. You should see something like the following screenshot:

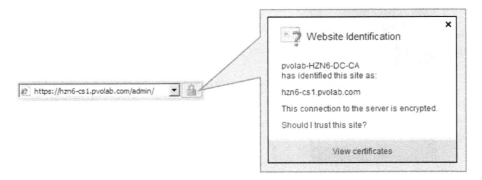

5. Now that we know that the certificate is in place, click on the **Login** button. You will now see the **VMware Horizon View Administrator** console page.

We will cover the console in more detail in *Chapter 5, A Guided Tour of the Horizon View Administrator Console.*

In the next section, we are going to install the remaining Horizon View components such as the security server, replica server, and then View Composer.

Installing the View security server

On the server that you are going to use as the security server, which is nondomain-joined, locate the installation software you downloaded previously into the shared network folder and launch the VMware-viewconnectionserver -x86_64-6.0.0-1884746 installation file. This is the same file we used to install the first connection server.

As the installation process is almost identical to that of the connection server, rather than showing every screenshot again, we will describe the process and show the screenshots where it is different.

> If you are connecting to the shared folder, you will need to enter your credentials to access it. This is because the security server is not joined to the domain. It is important that you don't join this server to the domain.

Again, note that the number at the end of the filename is the build number, and it might be different depending on the build or version of Horizon View you are installing.

After the installer application is launched, perform the following steps:

1. To start the installation, click on **Next >**.

2. In the **License Agreement** dialog box, accept the license agreement by clicking on the button for **I accept the terms in the license agreement**, and click on **Next >** to continue.

3. In the **Destination Folder** dialog box, click on **Change...** to change the installation folder, or click on **Next >** to accept the default location. In our example, we are going to stick with the default location. Click on **Next >** to continue.

4. The next dialog box is **Installation Options**, where we choose which type of connection server we want to install. The replica server and the security server are all different roles of the connection server.

As we are now installing the security server, select **View Security Server** from the list of options (**1**), as shown in the following screenshot:

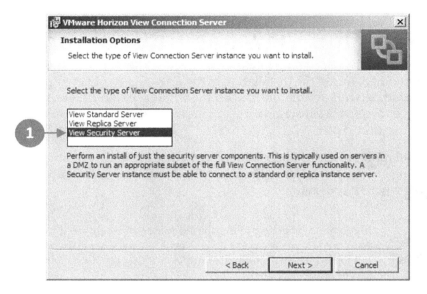

5. Click on **Next >** to continue.

6. In the next dialog box, we are going to pair our security server with our connection server that we installed in the previous section. First, we need to enter the hostname or IP address of our connection server (**2**). In our example lab, this is `hzn6-cs1.pvolab.com`:

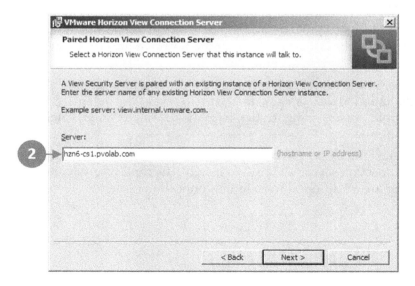

7. Click on **Next >** to continue and move to the **Paired Horizon View Connection Server Password** dialog box.

For the next step of the installation process, we need to quickly switch back to our connection server so that we can configure the pairing password.

From **View Administrator**, follow the steps as described:

1. Click on **Servers** from the left-hand side **Inventory** pane (**3**).
2. Click on the **Connection Servers** tab (**4**).
3. Select the connection server you want to pair with the security server. In our example, this is **HZN-CS1** (**5**).
4. Click on **More Commands** (**6**).
5. From the drop-down list, select **Specify Security Server Pairing Password…**(**7**).
6. This is shown in the following screenshot:

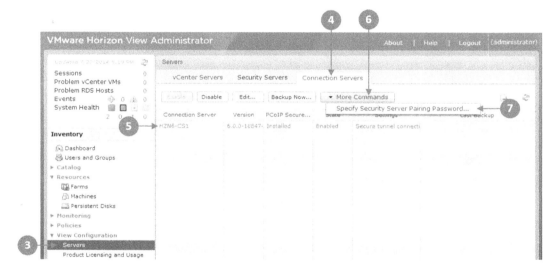

7. In the **Specify Security Server Pairing Password** dialog box, enter the following information:

    1. Enter the **Pairing password** value you want to use on the security server (**8**).
    2. Confirm the password you entered (**9**).
    3. Select a time period for the password (**10**).
    4. From the drop-down menu, choose **Minutes** or **Hours** for the password timeout (**11**).

This is shown in the following screenshot:

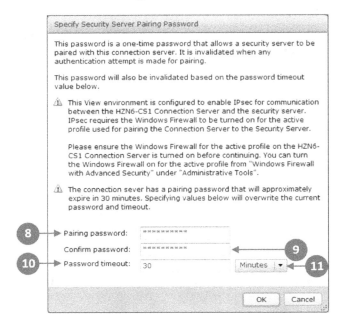

8. Once you have entered the information, click on **OK**.

9. Now, we can go back to the security server and enter the password we have just created so that we can pair it with our connection server.

10. Enter the pairing password in the **Password** box (**12**):

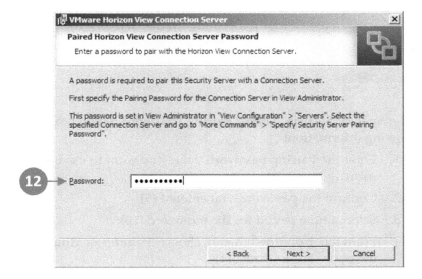

11. Click on **Next >** to continue.

In the **View Security Server Configuration** dialog box, we are going to configure the URLs that will be used for the end users to access their virtual desktop machines, when they are not connected to the internal network and are accessing via the Internet, for example. Configure the following parameters:

1. Enter the external URL. In our example, we have changed the URL to something more user friendly rather than the server name. Make sure that this name is still resolvable (**13**).

2. Enter the URL for the PCoIP external connection. This must contain an IP address (**14**).

3. Enter the URL for **Blast**. This is for HTML5 access to the desktop (**15**).

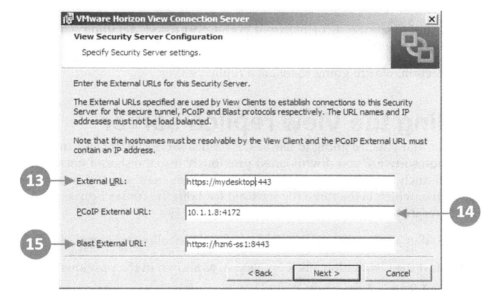

4. Click on **Next >** to continue.

5. In the **Firewall Configuration** dialog box, click on the radio button for **Configure Windows Firewall automatically**.

6. Click on **Next >** to continue.

7. In the **Ready to Install the Program** dialog box, click on **Install** to start the installation process for the security server. The security server is now installed. Once complete, click on **Finish**. If you want to view the readme files, then check the box for **Show the readme file** first.

8. You have now successfully installed the security server role. To check this, you can manage the security server, switch back to the **View Administrator** console, click on **Servers**, click on the **Security Servers** tab (**16**), and check whether the security server we have just installed is listed (**17**):

9. You should see the security server **HZN6-SS1** listed, detailing which connection server it is paired with.

In the next section, we are going to install a replica server.

Installing the View replica server

On the server that you are going to use as the replica server, locate and run the installation software you downloaded previously into the shared network folder, and launch the VMware-viewconnectionserver-x86_64-6.0.0-1884746 installation file, which is the same file we used for both the connection server and security server installation.

After the installer application is launched, perform the following steps:

1. To start the installation, click on **Next >**, as shown in the previous screenshot.

2. In the **License Agreement** dialog box, accept the license agreement by clicking on the button for **I accept the terms in the license agreement** and click on **Next >**.

3. In the **Destination Folder** dialog box, click on **Change...** to change the installation folder, or click on **Next >** to accept the default location. In our example, we are going to stick with the default location. Click on **Next >** to continue.

4. The next dialog box is for the **Installation Options**, where we choose which type of connection server we want to install. The replica server and the security server are all different roles of the connection server.

5. As we are now installing the replica server, select **View Replica Server** from the list of options (**1**), as shown in the following screenshot:

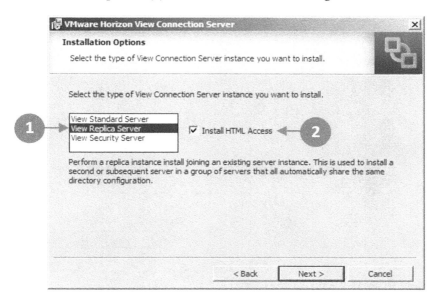

We also need to allow our users to have access to their virtual desktops machines from an HTML5 browser, so we need to tick the **Install HTML Access** (**2**) box (shown in the preceding screenshot). This needs to be configured in the same way as the first connection server, because if that server fails potentially, then this server will take over as the connection server. This might also be that due to the fact that the number of users in your environment exceeds the 2,000 limit of an individual desktop block, which means that you need more than one connection server.

6. Enter the address of an already existing connection server in the **Server:** box (**3**). This will be used to replicate the existing data:

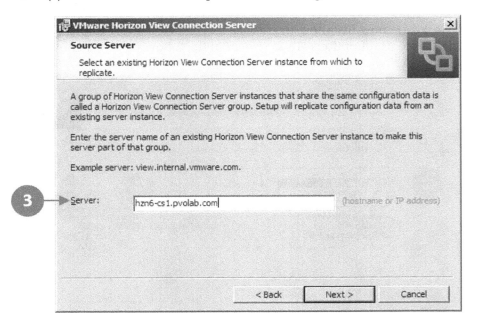

7. Click on **Next >** to continue.

8. As with the connection server, the **Firewall Configuration** dialog box allows you to automatically configure the Windows firewall ports that Horizon View requires in order to allow users to connect to their virtual desktop machines.

9. Click on the radio button for **Configure Windows Firewall automatically**.

10. Click on **Next >** to continue.

11. You are now ready to install the Horizon View replica server. Click on **Install** to start the installation.

12. Finally, if you want to read the readme file, then check the box; otherwise, click on **Finish** to complete the installation process and close the installation application.

13. You have now installed a second View Connection Server instance or replica server.

14. Click on **Finish**.

15. If we now switch back to our first and originally deployed connection server, we can make sure that the new instance has been recognized and is listed in the **View Administrator** console.

16. Click on **Servers** on the left-hand side of the **Inventory** pane (**4**), and then click on the **Connection Servers** tab (**5**):

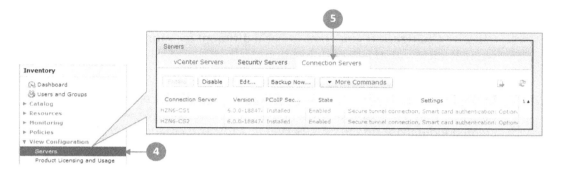

17. As per the previous screenshot, you will see the second connection server, which is **HZN6-CS2**, listed as one of the available connection servers.

In the next section, we are going to install the View Composer software.

Installing View Composer

The Horizon View Composer can be installed a vCenter Server or as a standalone service. If you are using **vCenter Server Appliance** (**VCSA**), then you will have to install the standalone version, as the VCSA is SUSE-based and View Composer is a Windows service. By being standalone, it also makes for better scalability.

Before you start the installation, you need to ensure that you have .NET 3.5 SP1 installed on your server and also the SSL certificate, as we will need this during the installation process. You will also need to set up a SQL database.

On the server that you are going to use as the View Composer server, locate the installation software you downloaded previously into the shared network folder, and launch the `VMware-viewcomposer-6.0.0-184350` installation file. This is the same file we used to install the first connection server.

Again, note that the number at the end of the filename is the build number, and it can be different depending on the build or version of Horizon View you are installing.

After the installer application is launched, perform the following steps:

1. In the **Welcome to the Installation Wizard for VMware Horizon View Composer** dialog box, click on **Next >** to start the installation.

2. Click on the radio button to accept the terms of the license agreement.

3. Click on **Next >** to continue.

4. Accept the default folder location for where View Composer will be installed. Click on **Change...** if you want to use a different location. In our example, we will stick with the default location.

5. Click on **Next >** to continue.

6. In the **Database Information** dialog box, enter the DSN name to the database that View Composer will use (**2**). In our example, we have created a database on our SQL Server already and created a DSN called View Composer. You can create the DSN from here by clicking on the **ODBC DSN Setup...** button.

7. Enter the username that you set when you created the DSN (**3**), and then enter the password for that user (**4**).

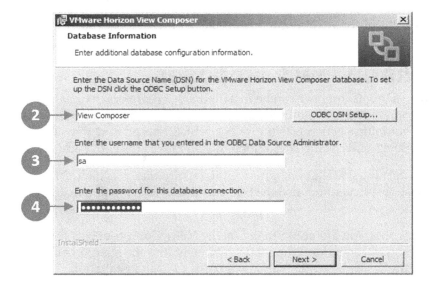

8. Click on **Next >** to continue.

9. In the **VMware Horizon View Composer Port Settings** dialog box, leave the **SOAP Port** value as the default setting (**5**). Click on the radio button for **Use an existing SSL certificate** (**6**), and then ensure that you click on the relevant certificate (**7**):

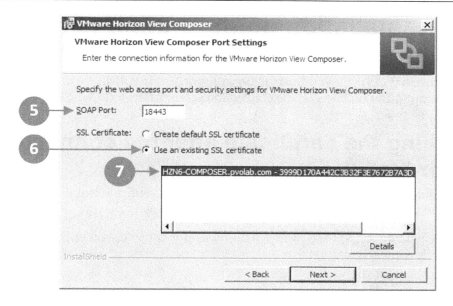

10. Click on **Next >** to continue.

11. In the **Ready to Install the Program** dialog box, click on **Install**.
    Once the View Composer has completed installing, click on **Finish**
    in the **Installer Completed** dialog box.

12. You are then prompted to restart your system. Click on **Yes** to reboot.

13. Once the server is back up and running, click on **Start** and then **Run**
    to check whether View Composer is running. Type `services.msc`
    into the **Run** box.

14. In the **Services** dialog box, scroll down till you find **VMware Horizon
    View Composer**, and ensure that the service has started (**8**):

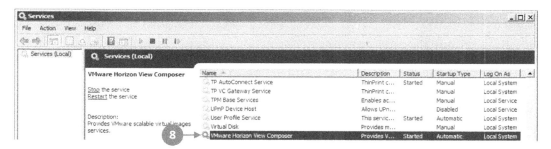

15. Close the **Services** dialog box.

Post-installation configuration tasks of the connection server

Now that we have our View infrastructure components installed, we are going to carry out some configuration tasks on the connection server in the following sections.

Installing the certificate after the connection server installation

You will soon know whether or not you have a valid certificate installed on your connection server. For this, complete the following steps:

1. When you log in to the **View Administrator** console, you will see the following warning box:

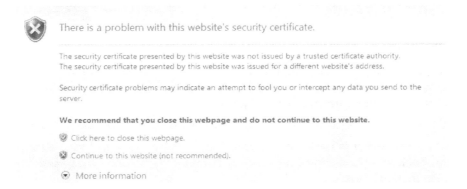

2. You will also see that the address bar shows **Certificate Error**:

3. Clicking on **Continue to this website (not recommended)** allows you to continue past the warning and log on to **View Administrator**. When you log on, you will see that there is a red warning box shown against **System Health**.

4. Click on the number below the red box (**1**). Then, click on the down arrow next to the **Connection Servers** menu (**2**), and then click on the connection server (**3**). In our example, the connection server is **HZN6-CS1**:

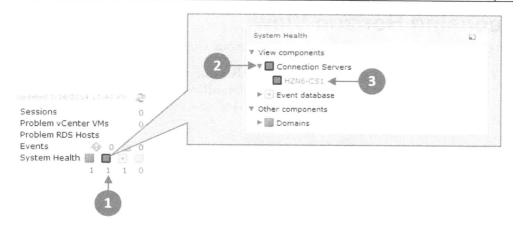

5. You will now see a dialog box that tells you that the certificate is not trusted:

6. Click on **OK** to close the dialog box.

Install the certificate in exactly the same way as described in the *Installing a certificate on the connection server* section of this chapter.

 After installing the certificate, you will need to restart the View Connection Server service in order for it to pick up the certificate.

Licensing Horizon View

One of the first things we need to do is license our Horizon View deployment:

1. When you first log in to **View Administrator**, you will see that it takes you to the **Licensing and Usage** page by default, as the product is currently unlicensed. Click on **Edit License...** (**1**) to add the license key:

2. Enter the license key into the box (**2**), and then click on **OK** (**3**):

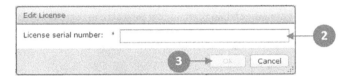

3. You will then see a dialog box confirming the license key has been added and what entitlements you have. In our example, we have a nonexpiring license for a concurrent user model that allows View Composer to be used. The application remoting license in disabled, so we know that this license is for the View standard edition:

The next thing we need to do is to add our vCenter Server, which we will do in the next section.

Adding vCenter Server and View Composer

The next stage of our installation and configuration is to add our vCenter Server to the **View Administrator** console, and then configure it to use View Composer. This can be done with the following steps:

1. Log in to **View Administrator**, and from the **Inventory** pane, click on **View Configuration** (1) and then on **Servers** (2).

2. Next, click on the **vCenter Servers** tab (3), and then click on **Add…** (4).

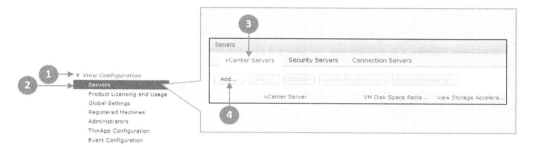

3. You will now see the **Add vCenter Server** dialog box, as shown in the following screenshot. We will now add the details of our vCenter Server. Enter **Server address** (5) followed by the vCenter Server **User name** (6) and **Password** (7). Add **Description** for what this vCenter Server is used for (8). Leave the **Advanced Settings** (9) section as default:

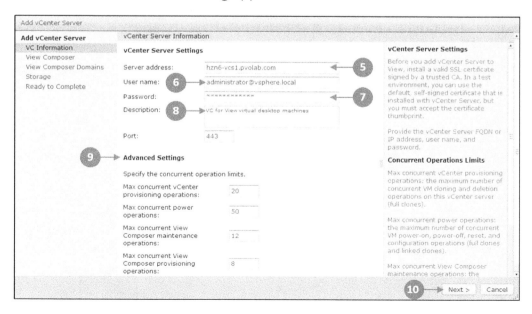

4. Click on **Next >** (**10**) to continue (shown in the preceding screenshot).

Next, we need to add the details of our View Composer server:

1. Click on the radio button for **Standalone View Composer Server** (**11**), enter the details in **Server address** (**12**), and then enter **User name** (**13**) and **Password** (**14**) of your service account that you set up for the composer service. In our example, we are using the same account as the one we used for vCenter.

2. Leave the **Port** setting (**15**) as default.

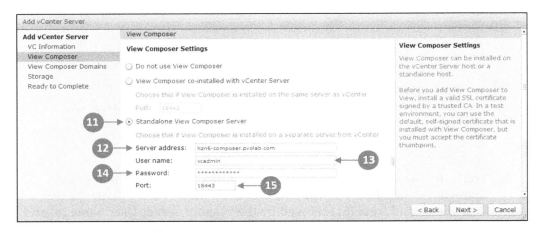

3. Click on **Next >** to continue.

Next, we need to add the domain details of where View Composer is going to create virtual desktop machines:

1. Click on the **Add...** button (**16**), and then enter the full name of your domain (**17**), followed by **User name** (**18**) and then **Password** (**19**). Click on **OK** when you are finished:

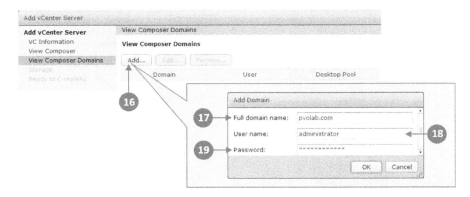

2. In the next settings box, we can enable some of the storage features available in the latest version of vSphere. Tick the box to turn on **Reclaim VM disk space (20)** and **Enable View Storage Accelerator (21)**, leaving **Default host cache size** as the default value:

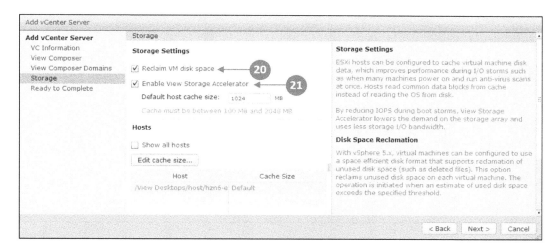

3. Click on **Next >** to continue.

One point to note is that if you get an error message saying that you are not running the latest version of vSphere and you know that you are, it's worth going back and checking whether you have entered your vCenter server credentials correctly. The configuration process doesn't check them when you enter them and move to the next page.

4. Finally, we are ready to complete the installation. Click on **Finish**:

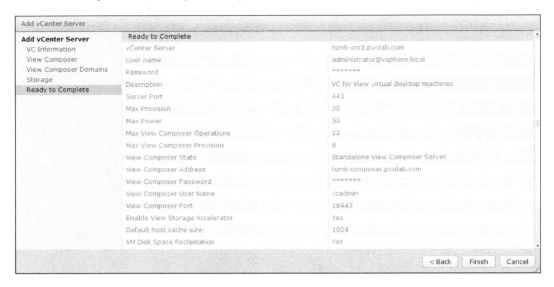

5. You should now see that you have successfully set up the connection to your vCenter Server and that View Composer is also set up:

View events database

Finally, we are going to add our View events database to the connection server so that we can start to record the events.

From the **System Health** section in the main **Dashboard** screen, you will see that the entry for **Event database (1)** has a yellow box next to it. This is because we have not yet configured it.

Click on the down arrow next to the **Event database** menu, and then click on **No events database configured** (2), as shown in the following screenshot:

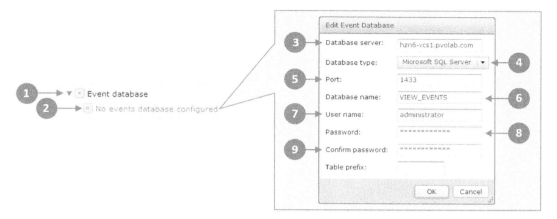

In the **Edit Event Database** configuration box, enter the details to connect to the SQL instance that is being used as the events database. In our example lab, we have created an instance called VIEW_EVENTS.

Enter the name in **Database server** (3), and then from the drop-down menu box (4), select the **Microsoft SQL Server** option The other option is for an **Oracle** database. Leave the **Port** setting as default (5).

Next, enter a name in **Database name** (6), followed by **User name** (7), and **Password** (8) for the service account that has access to the database. In our example, we are just going to use the administrator account. Enter the password again in the **Confirm password** box (9).

Click on **OK** when you have completed the configuration. You should now have a fully configured events database.

Summary

In this chapter, we downloaded and installed the different Horizon View components and configured the environment and made it ready in order to start preparing it for virtual desktop machines. We also looked at installing certificates and some tips on setting up both production and proof of concept environments.

In the next chapter, we are going to take a guided tour of **View Administrator** so that we become familiar with the web-based console, and when we move into the more-detailed configuration, you know where to find the various tasks and menu options.

5
A Guided Tour of the Horizon View Administrator Console

In this chapter, we are going to take a quick guided tour of the admin console that is used to drive the features and functions of Horizon View. We will cover some of the more common day-to-day tasks of managing a Horizon View infrastructure.

What is Horizon View Administrator?

The Horizon View Administrator is a web-based management console that is used to manage your View environment. It allows you to configure your infrastructure components as well as deploy your desktop pools and manage user entitlements.

Now that we have installed the connection server and other View infrastructure components (discussed in the previous chapters), we are going to connect to the View Administrator using the browser on our desktop.

To log in to the connection server, type the following URL into your browser:

```
https://hzn6-cs1.pvolab.com/admin
```

You will now see the login page displayed:

Log in using the administrator account and password, and select the domain from the drop-down menu. In our example, we are using the **PVOLAB** domain.

Horizon View Administrator console UI

Now that we have successfully logged in, we will see the **View Administrator** console interface. The **Dashboard** page is the default screen.

Dashboard

The **Dashboard** page gives you a quick, high-level snapshot of your entire View environment, as shown in the following screenshot:

On the **Dashboard** page, you can see the key things going on in your View environment, from system health and virtual desktop machine status to how much disk space is available in your datastores. You also have a number of options under the **Inventory** section.

We will take a closer look at these in the following sections of this chapter.

System Health

The **System Health** section displays the health of your individual View infrastructure components in the form of a traffic light system: green is good, yellow is a warning (degraded), and red means something serious is wrong.

In the following screenshot, we have expanded the **Connection Servers** menu by clicking on the arrow next to the entry (**1**). You will then see the list of all your connection servers, including their health status. If you click on one of them (we will click on **HZN6-CS1** (**2**) in this example) you will see a dialog box showing the details of any errors with that server:

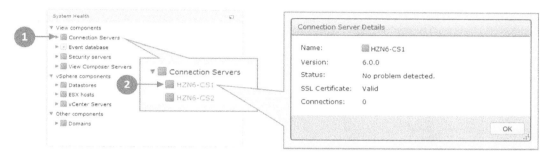

In this example, all is well with this particular server and everything shows as green. If it were red, then this dialog box would describe what the error is. You can also check all the other View infrastructure components along with your ESX host infrastructure and vCenter Servers, which (in this example) also shows the health as a green box.

Machine Status

The **Machine Status** box shows us what is happening with our virtual desktop machines categorized into **Preparing**, **Problem Machines**, and those that are **Prepared for Use**.

In the following screenshot, you can see the expanded **Preparing** folder (1):

You can then see that we get a finer level of detail and can see these virtual desktops that are in the **Provisioning** state or those that are being customized ready for use.

Datastores

The final box on the **Dashboard** screen shows us the datastore information. In this example, we have a single datastore and we can see that of the 32 GB total capacity that we have, 31 GB of disk space is still free:

Storage capacity is the key within a VDI environment as it can prevent new virtual desktop machines from being created, and therefore prevents users from working.

Inventory

On the left-hand side of the **View Administrator** console screen, you will see the **Inventory** box. This is where you will find all the tasks you need to configure and manage your View infrastructure:

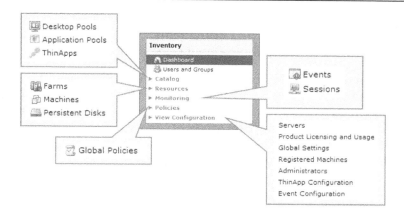

Let's take a closer look at these options and what each one is used for.

Users and Groups

The **Users and Groups** section displays what your users have been entitled to use and allows you to search the list and apply a filter (**2**) to help you search the entitled users if you have a large number of users. You can also change the filter type (**3**) to search on whether you want the results to contain, start with, or be an exact match of your search criteria.

The following screenshot shows the **Users and Groups** screen:

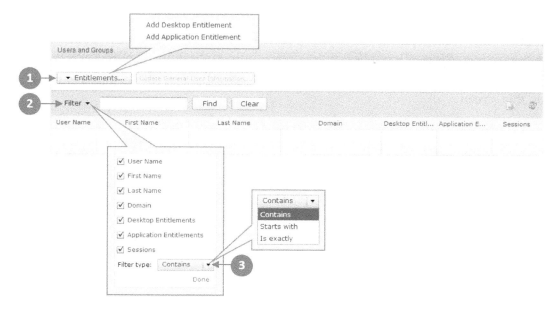

The other important task we can perform here is to entitle a user to either a desktop or an application. To do this, click on **Entitlements...** (1), as shown in the previous screenshot. A new **Add Desktop Entitlement** screen will be displayed.

From the **Domain** drop-down box (4), select the domain containing the user you want to entitle and then type in the name of that user (5). Click on **Find** (6) to locate the user. Highlight the username (7) and click on **Next**. You will then see a dialog box from which you can select the desktop pool. As we haven't created any desktop pools, this will be empty. We will cover desktop pool creation in detail in *Chapter 7, Configuring Horizon View to Deliver Virtual Desktops*:

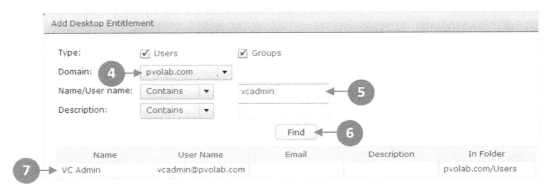

Catalog

The **Catalog** option allows you to build and configure your desktop pools, application pools in Horizon View Advanced Edition, and ThinApp entitlements.

As previously mentioned, building the actual desktop pools will be covered in detail in a later chapter. So for now, we will just take a look at the options available on this screen:

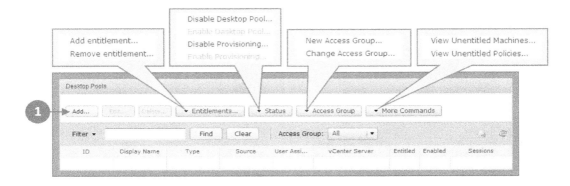

Clicking on **Add...** (1) will launch the configuration process for creating a desktop pool. We will discuss this in a later chapter. The following options are available:

- **Edit**: This edits an existing desktop pool configuration.
- **Delete**: This deletes an existing desktop pool.
- **Entitlements**: This adds or removes an entitlement to a desktop pool.
- **Status**: This enables or disables desktop pools as well as enabling or disabling the provisioning process.
- **Access Group**: This creates a new or changes an access group. Access groups allow you to delegate the administration of virtual desktop machines or desktop pools.
- **More Commands**: This shows us the unentitled machines and policies.

In the **Catalog** option, you can catalog **Application Pools** (Advanced Edition) and also a catalog of ThinApp-packaged applications.

Resources

The **Resources** option show the key resources of **Farms** (view published applications), **Machines**, and **Persistent Disks**. If we take a look at the **Machines** option, you can see the details of each one of the virtual desktop machines:

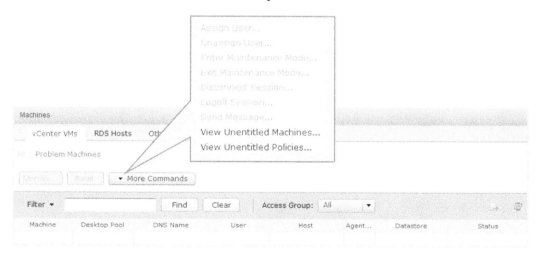

By clicking on **More Commands**, you can see that you can perform a number of actions on the virtual desktop machines. Simply highlight the machine on which you want to perform the action and then select what you want to do. For example, you might want to disconnect the users session or log them out.

Under the **Resources** option, you can also manage your persistent disk configurations and either detach an attached disk from a virtual desktop machine or import an existing disk from your vCenter. This option allows you to reattach a disk or VMDK file to a virtual desktop machine.

Monitoring

The **View Administrator** console allows you to monitor View events and View sessions that are stored in the View events database — one of the SQL Server databases that we require.

View events monitoring

View events monitoring allows you to monitor any event that happens within your View infrastructure. It is not only used for picking up errors and problems, but also records other activities and can provide an audit trail of performed tasks. Clicking on **Time period** (1) allows you to view events from last week, last month, or all events, as shown in the following screenshot:

View session monitoring

The second option allows you to monitor the View sessions; sessions that are both connected and being used and also those that are disconnected. Apart from this, you can also see information such as when a user logged on, how long they were connected for, and what they connected to so that you can also perform a number of actions, as shown in the following screenshot:

If you highlight the user/desktop you want to perform the action against, you can perform the following actions:

- **Disconnect Session** (**2**): This disconnects the user from their virtual desktop
- **Logoff Session** (**3**): This logs off the user
- **Reset Virtual Machine** (**4**): This reboots the virtual desktop machine
- **Send Message** (**5**): This sends a message to the user

Global Policies

The **Global Policies** option allows you to configure a global policy that is effective across all virtual desktop machines. By clicking on **Edit Policies...** (**1**), you can change the behavior of MMR, USB access, and PCoIP acceleration:

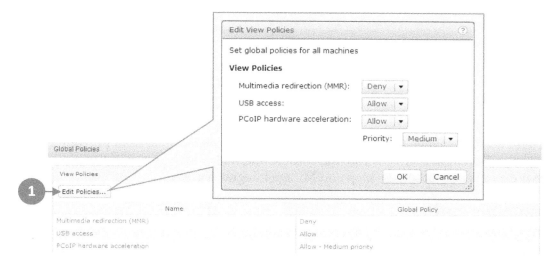

View Configuration

The **View Configuration** section is the main place where you configure the infrastructure. We have already taken a look at some of the items in this section in *Chapter 4*, *Installing Horizon View 6.0*, where we licensed the environment and then checked the **Servers** section to ensure the components were installed correctly.

Global Settings

In the **Global Settings** section, you can change the general settings within View. Click on **Edit...** (1) to edit the settings, as shown in the following screenshot:

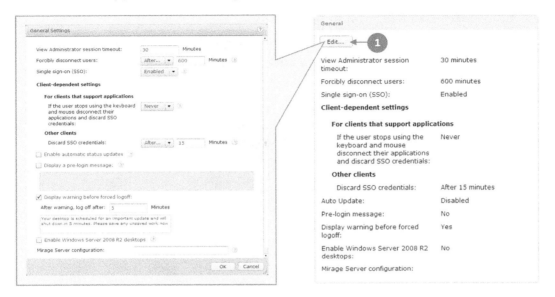

Here, you can change things such as the **View Administrator session timeout** setting, the length of time before the console automatically logs you out, or enable Windows Server-based desktop and Mirage integration.

Administrators

The **Administrators** section allows you to configure the user accounts that have administrative access and privileges within View. You can also define different roles.

If you click on **Administrators** from the **Inventory** box on the left-hand side, you will see the following screen:

Here, you can see we already have the administrator account added. We can add new users or groups by clicking on the **Add User or Group...(1)** button (shown in the preceding screenshot).

We can also add different roles to the different users as shown in the following screenshot:

Click on the **Roles** tab (**2**) and then click on **Add Role...** (**3**). You can either add a new role to a user or edit existing roles. You can use this to allow different administrator types or different levels of access. Maybe you configure a role where the user has just the ability to manage desktop pools and entitlements, or maybe they have access to installation and configuration tasks.

Event Configuration

The final section that we are going to briefly cover is **Event Configuration**. This allows View to store all of its events in either a SQL or Oracle database, and this is where you can configure this option and configure View to use an exiting database.

You can then configure how long you want to display the events for in the **View Administrator** console, as shown in the following screenshot. If you click on the **Edit...** button (**1**), you can then change the event settings:

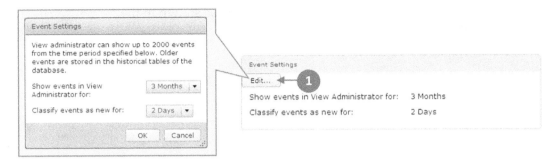

Summary

In this chapter, we took a closer look at the **View Administrator** console that is used to configure and manage your View infrastructure to deliver virtual desktop machines to your end users.

We covered some of the key parts of the **View Administrator** console. You should now be able to confidently navigate around the admin screen, locate various tasks, and be familiar with the layout of the console.

Now that we have our Horizon View infrastructure up and running and you are a bit more familiar with the admin console, we are now going to take a look at how to build virtual desktop machines for our end users in the next chapter.

6

Building and Optimizing Virtual Desktop Machine OS Images

With our Horizon View infrastructure now in place, it's time to turn our attention to the virtual desktop machines and look at how we can build an operating system image that is built and optimized to run as a virtual desktop machine.

In this chapter, we will cover some of the processes, best practices, and tools that will be used to create our virtual desktop images.

To build our virtual desktop machine, there are six steps that we are going to follow:

- Creating the virtual desktop machine in vCenter
- Installing the guest operating system
- Installing VMware Tools
- Optimizing the image for VDI
- Installing applications and the View Agent
- Creating a template/snapshot of the virtual desktop machine

There are a number of ways in which we can build the operating system, for example, using automated tools such as the Microsoft Deployment Kit, but in this example, we will perform a manual install using the installation media.

For our example lab, we are going to build two images, one for Windows 7 and the other for Windows 8. The reason is that we are going to look to deploy one image as a floating, linked clone desktop and the other as a dedicated desktop.

Creating the virtual desktop machine

The most obvious thing we need to do first is create a virtual desktop machine. For this, we will use our vCenter Server and once created, we will install the desktop operating system.

> Make sure that you don't simply convert a physical machine to virtual machine. A best practice is to create a brand new virtual desktop machine from the ground up. This way, you don't end up with physical-based elements in your image that might cause performance issues.
>
> Typically, a physical image will have been updated and patched numerous times and will have become bloated and might contain some old "rubbish". Virtualizing it means that we will end up with a bloated VM and virtualized rubbish.

Once we have our virtual desktop machine built and installed, we will run through the optimization process.

Creating the virtual machine in the vCenter Server

Log in to the vCenter Server using the vSphere Web Client with your administrator username and password, as shown in the following screenshot:

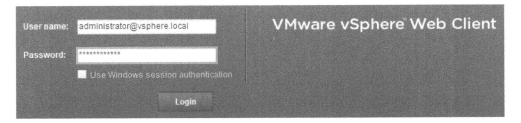

You will now see the home page. From here, we need to navigate to the data center or ESXi host server in order to create the first virtual desktop machine. To create the virtual machine in the vCenter Server, perform the following steps:

1. From the **Home** page, click on **Hosts and Clusters (1)**, and then expand the vCenter by clicking on the arrow. In our example, our vCenter is called **hzn6-vcs1.pvolab.com**.

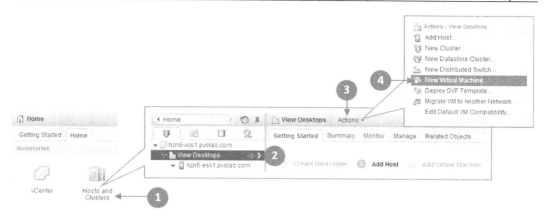

2. Highlight the **View Desktops** data center (**2**), and then click on **Actions** (**3**). Finally, select **New Virtual Machine…** from the menu (**4**).

> We are using the example lab infrastructure for this book, so feel free to create an ESX infrastructure that suits your needs, or use an existing platform and substitute any of these steps to reflect your own environment.

3. You should now see the **New Virtual Machine** dialog box, as shown in the following screenshot:

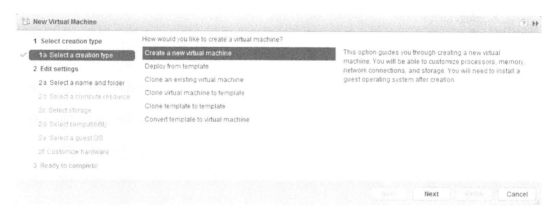

4. Click on **Next** to continue:

5. Type in a name for this virtual desktop machine (**1**), and then highlight the data center in which you want to create it (**2**). In our example, we will call this machine `Windows 7 Gold Image`. Click on **Next** to continue.

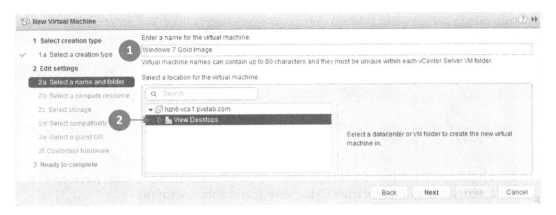

6. Select the resource where you want this virtual desktop machine to run. In this example, we will select our ESXi host, which is **hzn6-esx1.pvolab.com** (**3**).

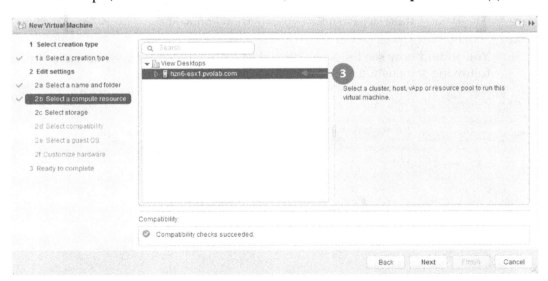

7. Click on **Next** to continue.

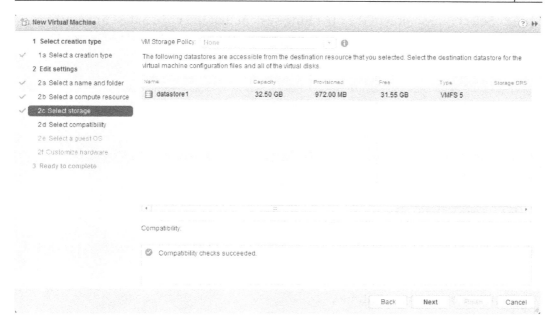

8. Select the datastore on which you want to store the virtual desktop machine. In our example lab, we only have one datastore.

9. Click on **Next** to continue.

10. Select the compatibility level for the virtual desktop machine (**4**). In our example lab environment, we have **ESXi 5.5** hosts, so we will use VM Version 10 to take advantage of all the features of this platform.

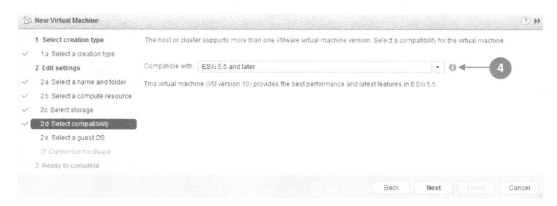

11. Click on **Next** to continue.

12. Select the version of the operating system that the virtual desktop machine is going to run. Choose the **Guest OS Family** (**5**) and **Guest OS Version** options (**6**) from the drop-down menus:

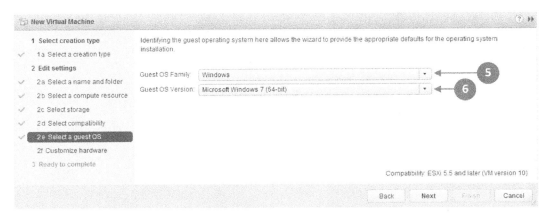

13. Click on **Next** to continue.

14. In the next screen, shown in the following screenshot, you can choose the hardware configuration of the virtual desktop machines. This is going to be dependent on your own specific use cases and what the desktop is going to be used for.

    In our example, we have pretty much left everything as default rather than reducing the capacity of the hard disk to suit our available storage.

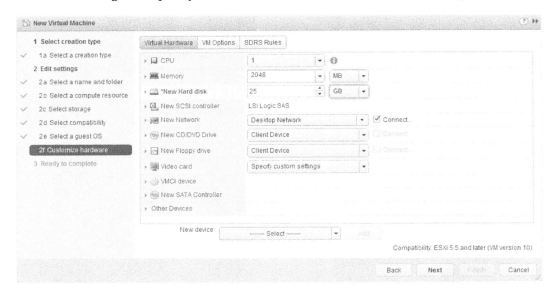

Leave the **Video card** settings as the default, as whatever you set here will ultimately be overridden by the settings from the desktop pool configuration from within View. You will be able to set the amount of VRAM and the 3D rendering from within the desktop pool settings.

15. Before you click on **Next**, click on the **VM Options** tab (7), as shown in the following screenshot:

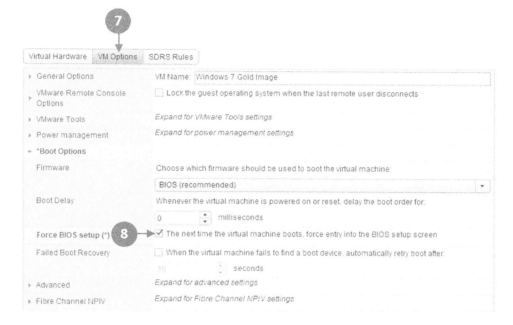

16. Check the box for **Force BIOS setup** (8) so that the virtual desktop machine boots up into the machine BIOS before we install the guest operating system.

    The reason for this is that we need to ensure that certain hardware components are switched off as they are not supported in a virtual desktop machine. Things such as LPT ports (printers), COM ports (serial), and floppy disk drives are not supported. We will cover this in the next section

17. Click on **Next** to continue.

18. On the next screen, which is **Ready to complete**, check that the settings are correct and accurately reflect the desired hardware configuration, and then click on **Finish**.

We have now built the container for the virtual desktop machine. The next step is to install the guest operating system. In this example, we will install Windows 7.

Configuring the virtual desktop machine BIOS

Before we get on with the guest operating system installation, we will cover how to make the BIOS changes required for the virtual desktop machine that we mentioned previously.

Updating the BIOS settings

The following steps will guide you through the process of updating the BIOS:

1. Power on the virtual desktop machine. From vCenter, highlight the virtual desktop machine — **Windows 7 Gold Image** (**1**) — right-click on it, and then select **Power On** (**2**).

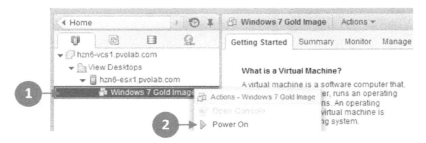

2. As the virtual desktop machine powers on, open a console on it. In vCenter. click on the **Summary** tab (**3**) for the virtual desktop machine, and then click on **Launch Console** (**4**).

The console will get launched as another browser window.

The virtual desktop machine will boot up into the BIOS screen on the first boot, so we can perform the BIOS configuration changes related to this being a virtual machine.

3. First, set the **Legacy Diskette A:** setting to **Disabled** (5) using the cursors in order to move down and highlight the option. Use the + and – keys to change the setting.

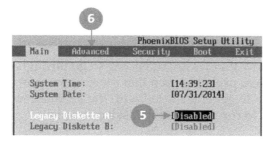

4. Move to the **Advanced** section (6) using the cursor keys and the right arrow.

5. Under the **Advanced** section, select **I/O Device Configuration** (7) and press *Enter*.

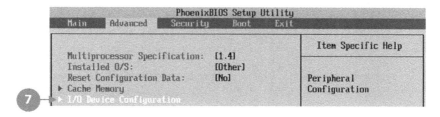

6. Set all the options (serial, parallel, and floppy disk) to **Disabled** (8).

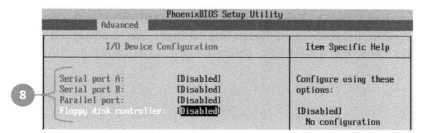

7. Once you have completed these changes to settings, press *F10* to save and exit. The virtual desktop machine will now reboot.

The reason we disable these components is due to the fact that this hardware does not exist in a virtual world; how it would behave is another aspect. Take the floppy drive, for example. A physical PC knows when you insert a disk, but in a virtual desktop, it doesn't. So, in order to check whether a disk has been inserted, it continually checks. This checking process takes up unnecessary resources that can impact the performance.

Starting the guest operating system installation

You'll be pleased to know that we are not going to go through a complete Windows 7 installation, as you have probably seen that more times than you care to remember, so the following steps will get you started with the installation before we move on to customizing the image to run as a virtual desktop machine.

With the virtual desktop machine powered on, we can start the guest operating system installation. Before we do this, we need to connect a virtual CD drive to the virtual desktop machine that contains the installation media for Windows 7.

From the vSphere Web Client and the **Summary** tab, click on the down arrow next to **CD/DVD drive 1 (1)**, and then select **Connect to CD/DVD image on a local disk... (2)**.

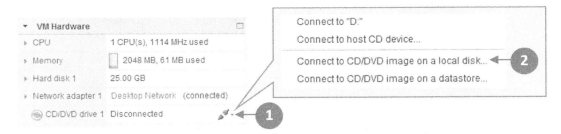

You will then see a dialog box where you can enter the location for the guest operating system installation media. In our example, we have copied the ISO for Windows 7 into the \\hzn6-dc\Shared Folder\Windows 7\ file share.

With the installation media connected, return to the console of the virtual desktop machine and reboot it by clicking on **Send Ctrl-Del-Delete (3)**.

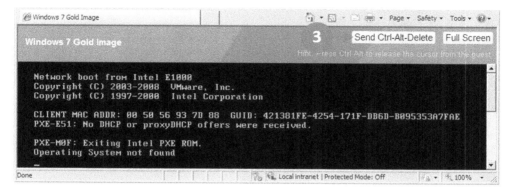

The virtual desktop machine will now reboot, connect to the CD drive, and start to load the Windows setup from the Windows 7 ISO. You should see the familiar **Starting Windows** screen.

We are not going to cover a Windows installation, so continue the Windows 7 setup until you have a virtual desktop machine running and joined to the domain. In the next sections, we will optimize and install the relevant tools required to make this a Horizon View desktop.

Installing VMware Tools

Now that we have a running virtual desktop machine, the next thing we need to do is install VMware Tools in the same way as we would for any other VMware-based virtual machine:

1. From the vSphere Web Client and the **Summary** tab, click on **Install VMware Tools (1)**.

2. In the **Install VMware Tools** dialog box, click on **Mount** (**2**) to attach the VMware Tools image to the virtual desktop machine.

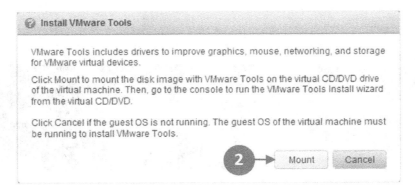

3. Switch back to the console of the virtual desktop machine.

4. You will see that the disk image has been mounted and the AutoPlay feature has kicked in. Click on **Run setup64.exe** to start the installation.

5. Click on **Yes** in the **UAC** dialog box, if displayed, to allow the installation program to make changes to the computer.

6. The **Welcome** screen for the installation wizard is now displayed. Click on **Next >** to start the installation.

7. In the **Choose Setup Type** dialog box, check the radio button for **Typical** (**4**).

8. Click on **Next >** to continue.

9. In the **Ready to install VMware Tools** box, click on **Install** to start the installation.

10. When the installation is complete, you will see the **Completed the VMware Tools Setup Wizard** box. Click on **Finish** to complete the installation.

11. You will then be prompted to reboot the virtual desktop machine. Click on **Yes** to reboot.

12. Once the virtual desktop machine starts up, check whether VMware Tools is running by looking at the system tray icon (**5**), as shown in the following screenshot:

In the next section, we will install applications, and then we will install the View Agent.

Installing applications and the View Agent

Before we install the View Agent, now is the time to install any applications that you want to include in your base image. These would be applications that every user needs access to, so applications such as Adobe Reader or the base level of Microsoft Office can be installed.

Once we have finished installing our applications, we can install the View Agent.

Browse the location where you have the View Agent. In our example lab, this file is in the \\hzn6-dc1\Shared Folder\View 6.0 shared folder.

Launch the installer and perform the following steps:

1. On the **Welcome to the Installation Wizard for VMware Horizon View Agent** screen, click on **Next >** to continue.

2. Click on the radio button for **I accept the terms in the license agreement**, and then click on **Next >**.

3. You will now see the **Custom Setup** screen, where you can choose which features are to be installed on the virtual desktop machine, as shown in the following screenshot:

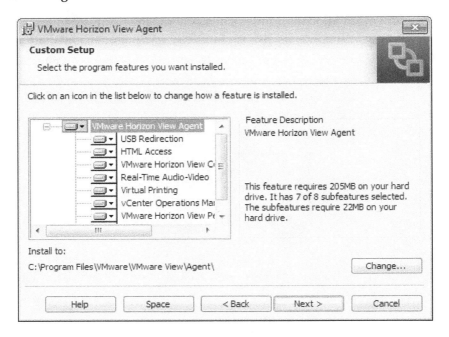

4. You can chose from the following options:
   ° **USB Redirection**
   ° **HTML5 Access**
   ° **VMware Horizon View Composer Agent**
   ° **Real Time Audio Video (RTAV)**
   ° **Virtual Printing**
   ° **vCenter Operations Manager Agent**
   ° **VMware Horizon View Persona Management Agent**
   ° **PCoIP Smartcard**

5. For our example installation, we will leave all the options as default but the **PCoIP Smartcard** support will be installed. Click on **Next >** to continue.

6. Click on the radio button for **Enable the Remote Desktop capability (2)**, and click on **Next >**.

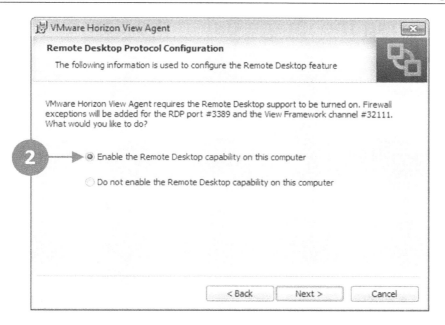

7. In the **Ready to Install the Program** box, click on **Install** to start the installation process. The View Agent will now be installed on the virtual desktop machine.

8. In the **Installer Completed** box, click on **Finish** to finalize the installation. You will be prompted to reboot. Click on **Yes** to reboot the virtual desktop machine.

You have now built a virtual desktop machine complete with VMware Tools and the View Agent installed.

The next stage is to optimize the machine we just built so that it runs as a virtual machine.

Optimizing the image

In this section, we are going to look at two ways of optimizing the virtual desktop machine. One is a manual, script-based process and the other uses an optimization application with a GUI-driven console. You might want to review what gets removed or switched off in order to ensure that the virtual desktop machine has the features you require and behaves as expected.

Optimizing the image using the commands.bat process

The `commands.bat` file is found as an attachment to the VMware View Optimization Guide, which can be downloaded from the VMware website using :`http://tinyurl.com/7rzfw6b`. Then, follow the next set of steps:

1. Once downloaded, open the document in Adobe Reader and save the embedded files as follows. Click on the paperclip icon (**1**) to show the document attachments.

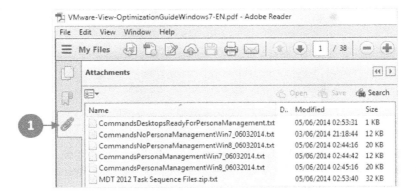

2. Right-click on the file you want to save, and click on **Save Attachment**. In this example, we are going to save the files to the `\\hzn6-dc1\Shared Folder\View 6.0\` shared folder. Repeat this for all of the attached files until they are saved in the shared folder.

    There are four key files that we need for optimization. There are two for Windows 7 and two for Windows 8. Then for each operating system version, there are two versions of the script, one for View Persona Management support, and one if you are not using View Persona Management. Now, switch back to the console of the virtual desktop machine.

3. Before we can run the optimization file, we first need to convert it into a `.bat` batch file rather than a `.txt` file. It's not just a case of renaming it.

4. Open the file using WordPad. You can use Notepad but beware that Notepad can introduce additional characters such as spaces that might prevent the file from executing.

5. With the text file open, you can make some changes to the script at this stage, should there be something specific that you want to change for your environment. In our example, we are going to keep the default customization options.

6. In WordPad, click on the down arrow in the top left-corner (**2**), and then click on **Save as** (**3**), followed by **Other formats** (**4**), as shown in the following screenshot:

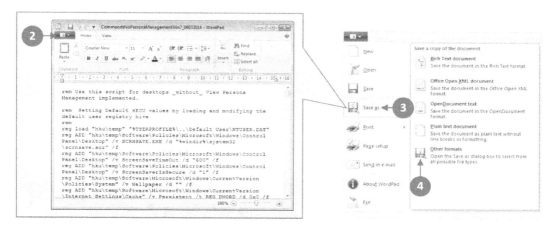

7. In the **Save As** box, type `"commands.bat"` (**5**), ensuring that you use quotes around the filename, as shown in the following screenshot:

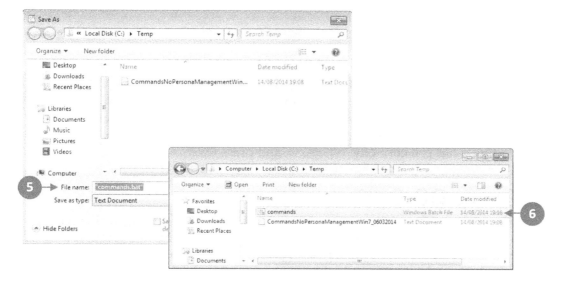

8. You should then see that it has now been saved as a `.bat` file (**6**) that can run as a script.

9. Close WordPad. We can now run our newly created script from the command line. In order to run the script correctly, you need to make sure that you run it with administrative privileges. You might already be logged in as the administrator, but just to make sure, we will run the **Run as administrator** option.

10. Navigate to **Start** | **All Programs** | **Accessories**, and then highlight **Command Prompt** (**7**). Right-click on **Command Prompt**, and then choose **Run as administrator** (**8**) from the menu, as shown in the following screenshot:

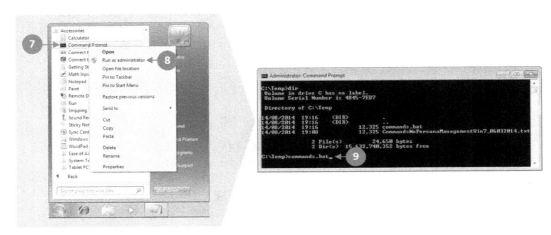

11. In the **Command Prompt** window, type commands.bat (**9**) and press *Enter*.

    The script will now run and might take a few minutes to complete. Once it has finished executing, scroll back through the window and check to make sure nothing has failed or there weren't any errors. When you are happy that it has run correctly, type exit and press *Enter*.

VMware OS Optimization Tool

The other option for optimizing the virtual desktop machine is using a GUI-based tool available from the VMware Labs website as a fling. In VMware terms, a fling is a free piece of software for people to try out and give feedback on to VMware. Often, these products make it into production, or form part, or become a feature of another product. The only thing to bear in mind that these product flings don't have any official support.

Download the tool and save it in the shared folder. You can download the tool from https://labs.vmware.com/flings/vmware-os-optimization-tool.

Let's take a few minutes just to see how this tool works.

VMware OS Optimization Tool is an application that you can execute on the virtual desktop machine that you are optimizing. It also has the ability to analyze and optimize remote systems.

From the Windows 7 virtual desktop machine, locate the application and launch it. You will see the following screenshot:

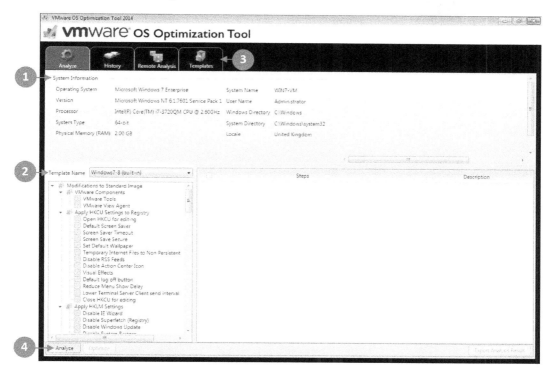

Let's take a look at the various sections:

- In the first section (**1**), you can see the details of the virtual desktop machine that shows the operating system and hardware configuration.

- The next section (**2**) is where you choose the template that you want to use for the optimization. You have the ability to create new templates using this tool by clicking on the **Templates** tab (**3**).

- To start the process, the tool firstly analyzes the differences between the current virtual machine state and the optimizations contained in the template. Click on **Analyze** (**4**) to start the process.

The tool will run the analysis and then come back with a report that shows you the components that need to be optimized. At this stage, you can select or deselect options before you actually run the optimization. Scroll through the analysis results to understand what is going to be changed.

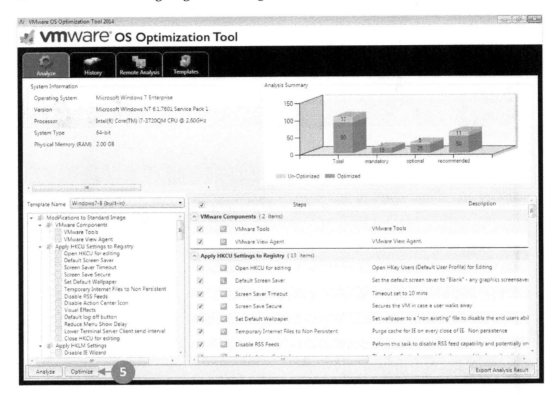

When you are happy, click on **Optimize** (**5**) to start the optimization process.

The image will not be optimized as per the setting and configuration contained in the template that you chose. Once the optimization is complete, exit the tool.

In the next section, we will look at what's next for our virtual desktop machine.

Post-optimization

One of the final things to do is release the IP address if you have been using DHCP so that when the new virtual desktop machines are created from this image, they will obtain a new IP address.

Open a command prompt and type `ipconfig /release`, as shown in the following screenshot:

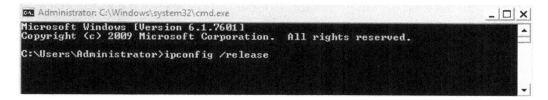

Before shutting down the virtual desktop machine and completing the build, there are a just a few housekeeping tasks to be performed.

Don't forget to tidy up behind you. For example, empty the recycle bin, delete any browser history or temporary files, and so on.

Once you are happy that the image is optimized to your requirements, you can shut down the virtual desktop machine. In the next section, we will prepare the image for delivery.

For our example lab, we are going to repeat the build and optimization process, but this time, we are going to build a Windows 8 virtual desktop machine.

In the next section, we are going to repeat the process again in order to build a third virtual desktop machine, but this time, we are going to build a GPU-enabled virtual desktop machine.

Building a GPU-enabled virtual desktop machine

In the previous sections, we discussed how to build a standard desktop image for Windows 7 and Windows 8 using standard virtual hardware components.

An advanced feature of Horizon View is the ability to use dedicated hardware installed in the ESX host servers, configured with PCI pass-through so that the virtual desktop machine can see the hardware. In this section, we are going to install an NVIDIA GRID GPU card and create a third virtual desktop machine image that has a dedicated assignment and access to the GPU resource using vDGA.

 vDGA requires a dedicated virtual machine assignment and, therefore, you will have a 1:1 mapping between virtual desktop machine and GPU.

Configuring the ESXi host and vCenter Server

Before you build the virtual desktop machine, you will need to have graphics cards installed into the ESXi host in preparation for building new virtual desktop machines that are configured to use the graphics cards.

In our example lab, we are using NVIDIA GRID K2 cards. These cards are available via the OEM route and come ready and configured from the server vendors due to them requiring additional power, cooling, and specific BIOS settings.

It's worth checking this before you start the configuration, as just retro-fitting the cards to an existing server might mean that they do not work.

With the hardware installed, log in to the vSphere Web Client, and navigate to the host into which the cards have been installed.

Click on the **Manage** tab (**1**), and then click on the **Settings** option (**2**), as shown in the following screenshot:

Expand the **Hardware** section (**3**), and click on **PCI Devices** (**4**). In the main screen, click on the pencil icon (**5**) to edit the settings, as shown in the following screenshot:

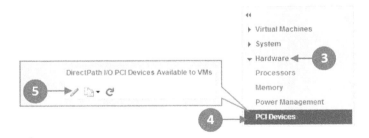

You will now see the following screenshot, showing you the device availability. In our example, we have a Supermicro X9DRG-HTF+ server configured with two NVIDIA GRID K2 cards. Check the boxes for the two GPU cards (**6**), as shown in the following screenshot, and then click on **OK**:

Building the virtual desktop machine

Next, we need to build the virtual machine. We will follow the steps as we previously described in this chapter in order to build a virtual desktop machine up to the point where we configure the virtual hardware, as now we need to add the GPU card at this point.

 To make use of this feature, the hardware version of this virtual desktop machine should be hardware Version 9 or higher.

In the **2f Customize Hardware** section and under the **Virtual Hardware** tab, click on the drop-down arrow (**1**) for **New device**, and from the list of options, click on **PCI Device** (**2**). Click on **Add** (**3**) to add the new device.

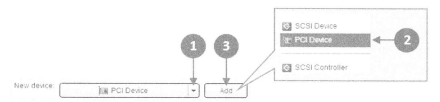

You will now see the following dialog box. Select one of the two NVIDIA cards from the drop-down box. The information warning around some of the operations that are not available to the virtual desktop machine is also worth noting.

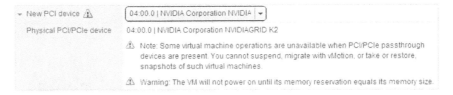

With the additional hardware and the NVIDIA card added (**4**) in the **Virtual Hardware** section, the final thing is to ensure that the box is ticked for **Reserve all guest memory (All locked)** (**5**), as shown in the following screenshot:

If you do not configure the memory reservation, then the virtual desktop machine will fail to power on.

You will also need to follow these mentioned steps for each vDGA-enabled virtual desktop machine you want to create and build. This is because each virtual desktop machine needs its own unique dedicated GPU memory address assigned to it.

The final step in the building of the virtual desktop machine process is to add an entry to the virtual machine configuration file (a VMX file). This is only a requirement if your virtual desktop machine has more than 2 GB of memory configured.

Edit the VMX file and add the `pciHole = "2048"` line, as shown in the following screenshot:

```
pciHole.start = "2048"
pciPassthru0.present = "TRUE"
pciPassthru0.deviceId = "11bf"
pciPassthru0.vendorId = "10de"
pciPassthru0.systemId = "51baead3-61b2-2958-6a0d-90b11c18c094"
pciPassthru0.id = "07:00.0"
pciPassthru0.pciSlotNumber = "192"
```

The next step is to install the operating system.

Installing the operating system for GPU-enabled desktops

In our example, we are going to build a Windows 7 virtual desktop machine for our high-end graphics. To install the operating system, follow the steps described in the *Creating the virtual machine in the vCenter Server* section of this chapter, but with one difference.

After you have installed the Horizon View Agent, you need to install the NVIDIA drivers in the virtual desktop machine. The drivers can be downloaded from `http://tinyurl.com/mzf2b33`

When you install the NVIDIA driver software, make sure that you select all components to be installed and not the **Express** option. **Express** will miss out on some of the key components that can be run in a virtual desktop machine.

Once you have the drivers installed, complete the operating system setup by installing any additional applications and then performing the optimization steps. It's probably worth checking whether the graphics card has been installed correctly by checking in the **Device Manager** of the virtual desktop machine, as shown in the following screenshot:

You should now have a GPU-enabled virtual desktop image ready to be prepared for delivery to the end users, which we will cover in the following sections of this chapter.

Due to the nature of these virtual desktop machines, the best way to deploy additional machines is by cloning the virtual desktop machines, and then making sure that each one is assigned to its own GPU resource.

Preparing the image for users

We now have our virtual desktop machine built, optimized, and ready for our users. The next stage of the process is to prepare the image and make it ready for View to deliver as either a full-clone desktop or a linked-clone desktop. The process for each delivery mechanism is subtly different.

Creating a template for a full-clone virtual desktop machine

To use this virtual desktop machine as a parent virtual desktop machine for your full-clone desktops, you will need to convert it to a virtual machine template using vCenter and the vSphere Web Client. Once you have completed this, you can then use the **View Administrator** console to create new virtual desktop machines from this template for a full-clone desktop pool.

In our example lab, we will use the Windows 8 image as create a full-clone, dedicated desktop pool based on that image.

Log in to the vSphere Web Client, and then perform the following steps:

1. Navigate to the **Windows 8 Gold Image** virtual desktop machine (**1**), and right-click on it.
2. Then, from the menu, click on **All vCenter Actions** (**2**).
3. Select the **Convert to Template** option (**3**). This is shown in the following screenshot:

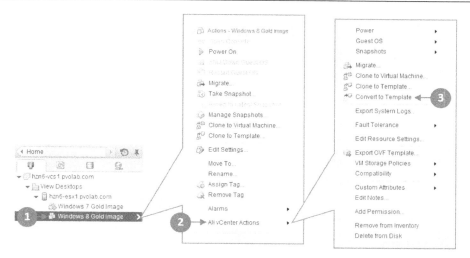

The virtual desktop machine is then converted to a template and is ready to be deployed.

Creating a snapshot for linked clones

To use this virtual desktop machine as a parent virtual desktop machine for your linked-clone desktops, you will need to take a snapshot of the virtual desktop machine using vCenter and the vSphere Web Client. Once you have taken the snapshot, it can be used by **View Administrator** to create new virtual desktop machines for a full-clone desktop pool. This will be used to create the replica in View Composer.

In our example lab, we will use the Windows 7 image and create a linked-clone desktop pool based on that image:

1. Log in to the vSphere Web Client, and navigate to the **Windows 7 Gold Image** virtual desktop machine (**1**). Right-click on it and select **Take Snapshot...** (**2**).

2. In the **Take VM Snapshot for Windows 7 Gold Image** box shown in the following screenshot, type in a name for the snapshot (**3**), and then give it a description (**4**):

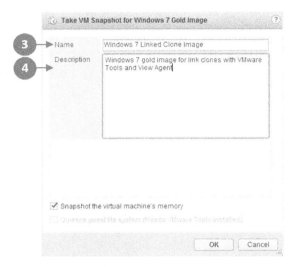

3. Click on **OK** when you are ready to take the snapshot. The snapshot is now created.

4. To check whether the snapshot has been taken, let's have a look at the snapshot manager. From the vSphere Web Client, highlight the **Windows 7 Gold Image** virtual desktop machine (**5**). Click on **All vCenter Actions** (**6**), **Snapshots** (**7**), and then select **Manage Snapshots...** (**8**).

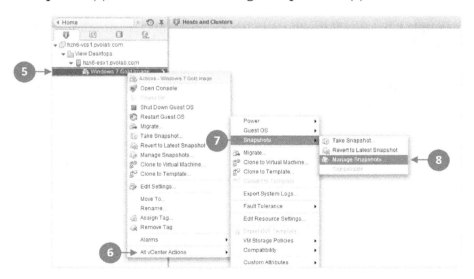

5. You will now see the **Manage VM Snapshots for Windows 7 Gold Image** dialog box where you should be able to see the snapshot that we have just taken (**9**).

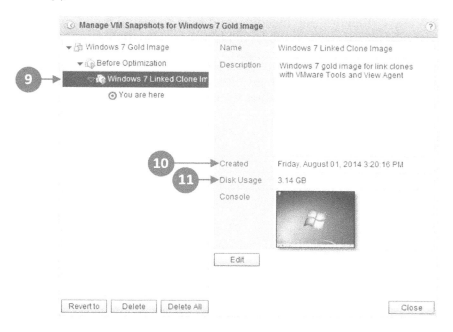

6. You can also see when the snapshot was taken (**10**) and the amount of disk space that it is consuming (**11**).

Preparing the GPU-enabled virtual desktop machine

As we discussed previously, the GPU-enabled virtual desktop machines are going to have a dedicated assignment, and each one should be built using the template feature of vCenter Server. We will then create a manual pool in the next chapter to deliver these virtual desktop machines to the end users.

Summary

In this chapter, we built our virtual desktop machine images that will act as our gold image or parent image, installed the operating system, optimized it to run as a Horizon View virtual desktop machine, and then prepared it and made it ready to be delivered to the end users. In total, we built three virtual desktop parent images.

In the next chapter, we will configure the **View Administrator** console and create our desktop pools and make them ready for our end users to connect and start using the virtual desktop machines that we just built.

7
Configuring Horizon View to Deliver Virtual Desktops

Our Horizon deployment so far consists of a couple of different elements, the View infrastructure components and a virtual desktop machine image that we have built in the previous chapters. It's now time to bring the two elements together so that View can deliver the virtual desktop machines to the end users.

In this chapter, we are going to configure and prepare Horizon View using the Horizon View Administrator to deliver virtual desktop machines by creating **desktop pools**.

In our example lab, we will configure three desktop pools—one for Windows 7 (floating assignment with linked clones), one for Windows 8 (dedicated and full clones), and finally a manual pool with a dedicated assignment, and using virtual desktop machines with an NVIDIA GPU.

Configuring a linked-clone desktop pool

The first desktop pool we are going to create is a linked-clone pool with a floating assignment based on our Windows 7 gold image. In the following sections, we are going to cover the desktop pool configuration process:

1. From the View Administrator console, click on **Desktop Pools** (**1**) in the **Inventory** section and then click **Add...** (**2**), as shown in the following screenshot:

2. You will now see the first of the **Add Desktop Pool** configuration pages, as shown in the following screenshot.

3. In this example, we are going to create an automated pool, so click on the radio button for **Automated Desktop Pool** (**3**), as shown in the following screenshot:

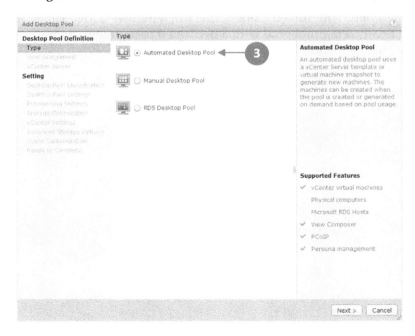

This option allows us to use the Windows 7 gold image snapshot to create machines on demand or provision up front, depending on what we choose.

The **Manual Desktop Pool** option allows you to create a pool consisting of machines such as other vCenter-based virtual machines or physical desktops.

Finally on this page, you can configure an **RDS Desktop Pool** that allows you to create a pool consisting of RDS desktop sessions managed by the View Connection Server.

4. Click on **Next** to continue to the next configuration screen.

5. On the **User Assignment** page, we can configure how the virtual desktop machines in this desktop pool will be assigned to the end users. The **Dedicated** options specify that the user will connect to the same machine each time they log on and effectively own that particular virtual desktop machine. If you select **Enable automatic assignment**, View will automatically assign a spare machine to that user if they do not already have a machine in that desktop pool.

> In our example lab, we are going to create a desktop pool that has a floating assignment, which means that virtual desktop machines are chosen at random when the user logs on.

6. Click on the radio button for **Floating (4)**, as shown in the following screenshot:

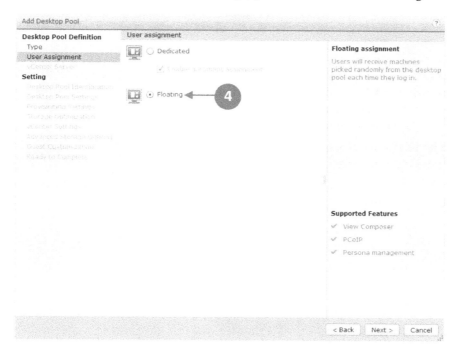

7. Click on **Next** to continue to the next configuration screen to configure vCenter Server:

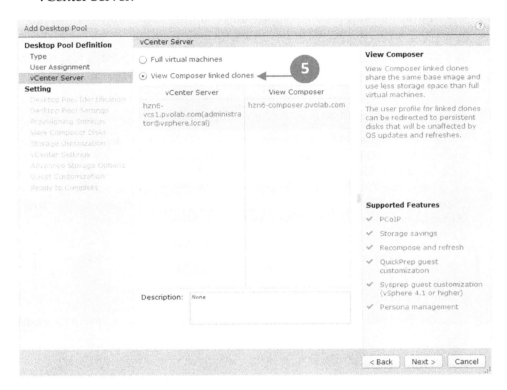

8. As this desktop pool is going to be a linked-clone pool, click on the radio button for **View Composer linked clones** (5), as shown in the previous screenshot. You will see that the vCenter Server and View Composer details have automatically been added.

9. The **Full virtual machine** option will create a complete copy of the virtual machine template on your vCenter Server.

10. Click on **Next** to continue to the next configuration screen and move on to the **Setting** section and the **Desktop Pool Identification** configuration.

11. On this page, we will give the desktop pool a unique name or **ID (6)**. For our example, we will give it the ID `Win_7_Floating_LC`. Note that you can't use spaces for the ID:

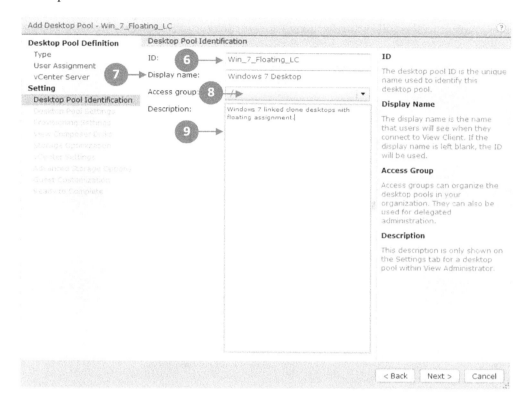

12. Enter a **Display name (7)**. Bear in mind that this is the name that users will see, so it's worth calling it something that is easily identifiable rather than something complicated. You can assign this pool to an **Access group (8)** that allows you to organize your desktops or to permit delegated administration.

13. Lastly, enter a **Description (9)** for this desktop pool. This is optional.

14. Click on **Next** to continue to the **Desktop Pool Settings** configuration page.

15. There are a number of settings that you can configure on this page and you will find these grouped under **General (10)**, **Remote Settings (11)**, **Remote Display protocol (12)**, **Adobe Flash Settings for Sessions (13)**, and **Mirage Settings (14)**. You will also find a number of settings in each of these groups, shown in the following screenshot:

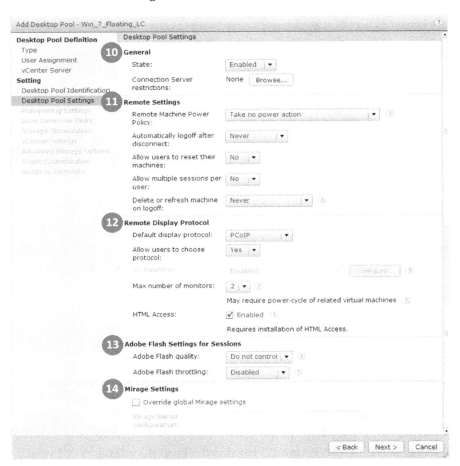

General

The **General** sections allows you to change the **State** of the pool to either **Enabled** or **Disabled**. Disabling a desktop pool containing desktops that users are entitled to means that they will no longer be able to connect to their virtual desktop machine. **Connection Server restrictions** allows you to configure tags, meaning that a desktop pool can only be accessed by connection servers that have specific tags assigned to them.

Remote Settings

The **Remote Settings** section defines how a virtual desktop machine behaves during a log-on and log-off operation.

- **Remote Machine Power Policy**: This governs the power-on policy for a virtual desktop machine. You have the following options:
    - ○ **Take no power action**: This does not perform any action
    - ○ **Ensure machines are always powered on**: This option enables machines to be powered on and ready to be allocated to the end users
    - ○ **Suspend**: This suspends the virtual desktop machine
    - ○ **Power off**: This powers off the virtual desktop machine

- **Automatically Logoff after disconnect**: This governs whether or not the user gets logged out of their virtual desktop machine when they disconnect. You have the following options:
    - ○ **Immediately**: This logs the user out as soon as they disconnect.
    - ○ **Never**: This always leaves the user logged in when they disconnect.
    - ○ **After**: This logs the user out after a period of time that you enter for this option. The default time is 120 minutes.

- **Allow users to reset their machines**: You can set this to **Yes** or **No** depending on whether you want users to do this.

- **Allows multiple sessions per user**: **Yes** allows multiple sessions and **No** means that the users are limited to just a single session.

- **Delete or refresh machine on logoff**: This determines what happens to the virtual desktop machine when the user logs off. These are the basic functions of using linked clones and you have the following options that reflect this:
    - ○ **Never**: This leaves the virtual machine in its current state
    - ○ **Delete Immediately**: This deletes the linked clone that was created
    - ○ **Refresh Immediately**: This refreshes the linked clone and results in a new Vanilla-linked clone being created

Remote Display Protocol

The **Remote Display Protocol** section defines the behavior of the desktop pool for the chosen protocol with the following options:

- **Default display protocol**: This allows you to choose which protocol View should be used by default. You have the choice of **PCoIP** or **RDP**.

- **Allow users to choose protocol**: This allows the user the choice of which protocol to use. You would typically set this to **No** and then set the default protocol to **PCoIP**. However, you might have users that travel and connect from various locations. You might find that ports could be blocked, specifically the UDP port 4172 that PCoIP uses to send the pixels from your desktop. You will soon know whether or not this is the case. When you connect to your virtual desktop machine, the login process goes smoothly and seems to work; however, your are then presented with a black screen. The reason is that the pixels can't get out to your client. Switching to RDP means that you can continue to use your virtual desktop machine.

- **Max number of monitors**: You can choose 1, 2, 3, or 4 monitor support.

- **Max resolution of any one monitor**: This allows you to set the maximum resolution. You can choose **1680x1050**, **1920x1200**, or **2560x1600**.

- **HTML Access**: Tick this option to enable desktops in this pool to be accessed via a browser.

Adobe Flash Settings for Sessions

The **Adobe Flash Settings for Sessions** section defines how a virtual desktop machine behaves during the log-on and log-off operation. You can set the **Adobe Flash quality** to the following:

- **Do not control**: This allows the web page to determine the best setting
- **Low** (default): Low quality means less bandwidth consumption
- **Medium**: Medium quality means average bandwidth consumption
- **High**: High quality means more bandwidth consumption

The other configurable setting is for **Adobe Flash throttling**. Adobe Flash updates the screen by default using a timer service to determine the update interval. By changing this time interval setting, you can control the frame rate of the screen updates and therefore reduce the bandwidth requirements. You can configure the following settings:

- **Disabled**: Throttling is turned off
- **Conservative**: The update interval is set to 100 ms

- **Moderate**: The update interval is set to 500 ms
- **Aggressive**: The update interval is set to 2,500 ms

Mirage Settings

The **Mirage Settings** section allows you to over-ride the Mirage global settings. In our example, we are going to stick with the default settings. Click on **Next** to continue to the **Provisioning Settings** configuration page.

As with the previous settings group, there are again a number of settings that you can configure on this page, and you will find these grouped under **Basic**, **Virtual Machine Naming**, **Desktop Pool Sizing**, and **Provisioning Timing**. You will also find a number of settings in each of these groups that we will discuss next:

- **Basic (15)**: This checks the **Enable provisioning** and **Stop provisioning on error** boxes and prevents the View Composer from carrying on if it encounters an error rather than going on and building hundreds of faulty virtual desktop machines.

- **Virtual Machine Naming**: This is where you give the virtual desktop machines their computer name as they are provisioned. You can specify the machine names manually by entering them as a list or you can use a naming pattern, as in our example.

  Click on the radio button for **Use a naming pattern (16)** and then enter the pattern you want to use for naming in the **Naming Pattern** box **(17)**. In our example, we are going to use a unique number in our machine name; enter Win7-vm{n}. The {n} part denotes the unique number, so the first virtual desktop machine that gets built will be called Win7-vm1, the second will be called Win7-vm2 and so on.

- **Desktop Pool Sizing**: In this section, you can define the number of virtual desktop machines this pool will consist of. Enter a value in **Max number of machines (18)** for this pool. In our example, we use 5.

  Now enter a value in **Number of spare (powered on) machines (19)**. This is the number of machines built ready for a user to connect to. We will just configure one spare machine.

  Finally, enter a value in **Minimum number of ready (provisioned) machines during View Composer maintenance operations (20)**. This allows a minimum number of virtual desktop machines to be available when you perform maintenance tasks on the View Composer and View Composer is not available.

- **Provisioning Timing**: There are two options in this section. First, click on the radio button for **Provision machines on demand** (**21**). This means that virtual desktop machines will be provisioned as end users logon and request a desktop. We will set the value of **Min number of machines** to 1 (**22**). This means there will always be one machine built ready. You may want to increase this number to take into account busy periods so that more machines are built up front.

The **Provision all machines up-front** option does exactly that. It builds all your linked clone virtual desktop machines prior to users requesting them.

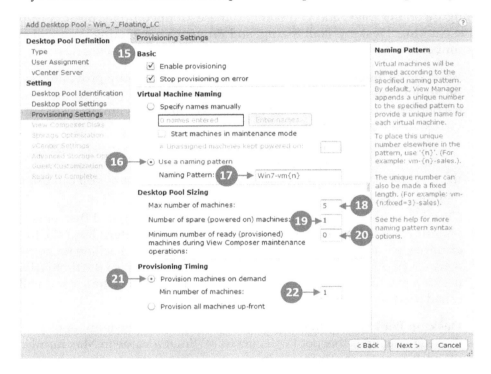

When using this option, beware that, if you have asked for 1,000 desktops and then set it to provision upfront, this will slow the infrastructure down as it builds all 1,000 machines. It's not advisable to do this in the middle of the day when users are using the infrastructure. In addition, the build task needs to complete within the time limit of 120 minutes. So, this is where fast storage comes into play and we use our assessment data to rectify the size of the storage platform.

Best practice would be to build a few virtual desktop machines at a time.

Click on **Next** to continue to the **View Composer Disks** configuration page. On this configuration page, you can choose what to do with disposable files. You can either redirect disposable files to a nonpersistent disk, which means they automatically get deleted when the user ends the session, or you can leave the files on the virtual machines hard disk. Best practice would be to redirect to a non-persistent disk, as there is no need to keep these files once the user has logged off.

In our example, click on the radio button for **Redirect disposable files to a non-persistent disk (23)**, as shown in the following screenshot:

Click on **Next** to continue to the **Storage Optimization** configuration page.

Click on the radio button for **Select separate datastores for replica and OS disks (24)**. This allows you to tier your storage and place replicas on fast SSD.

Click on **Next** to continue to the **vCenter Settings** configuration page. On this configuration page, we are going to configure vCenter so that it uses the Windows 7 gold image that we built in *Chapter 6, Building and Optimizing Virtual Desktop Machine OS Images*, and also where the newly built virtual desktop machines are going to be hosted.

There are seven sections to configure, as shown in the following screenshot. We will cover in more detail how to configure these.

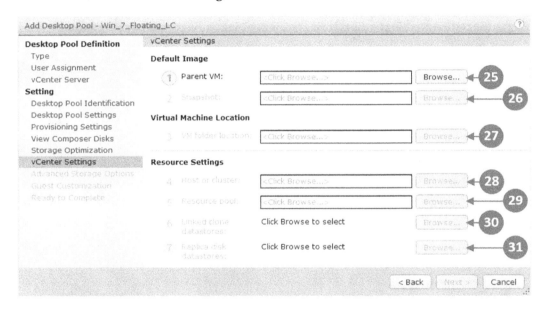

In the **Default Image** option, we will configure vCenter or the Windows 7 gold image.

We will start by configuring the **Parent VM**. Click on **Browse (25)**. You will see the following dialog box:

Select the parent VM you want to use for the machines in this pool. In our example, it's the **Windows 7 Gold Image**. Click on **OK** to return to the **vCenter Settings** page. Next, we will configure the **Snapshot**. Click on **Browse (26)** next to **Snapshot**, as shown in the following screenshot:

Select the **Win7 Gold Image** snapshot, as shown in the previous screenshot, and then click on **OK** to return to the **vCenter Settings** page.

In the **Virtual Machine Location** dialog box, we will configure the folder into which the virtual desktops will be deployed to.

Click on **Browse (27)** next to **VM folder location**. You will see the following dialog box:

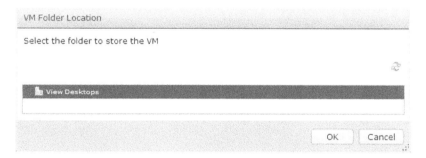

Select the folder you want to use. In our example, we are going to use the **View Desktops** folder. Click on **OK** to return back to the **vCenter Settings** page.

In our example, we configured the virtual desktop machines to be created at the datacenter level. It's a good practice to use vCenter folders to store the virtual desktop machines in so that by having a folder structure you can manage them in a better way.

In the **Resource Settings** section, we are going to configure the details of our infrastructure, host servers/clusters, and datastore information.

Click on **Browse (28)** next to **Host or cluster**. You will see the following dialog box:

Select the host server you want to use. In our example, we are going to use the **hzn6-esx1.pvolab.com** host server. Click on **OK** to return to the **vCenter Settings** page.

Click on **Browse (29)** next to **Resource pool**. Select the resource pool to use for these virtual desktop machines. In our example, we will use **hzn6-esx1.pvolab.com** as our host server because we don't have a resource pool configured.

Click on **OK** to return back to the **vCenter Settings** page.

Click on **Browse (30)** next to **Linked clone datastores**. You will see the following screenshot:

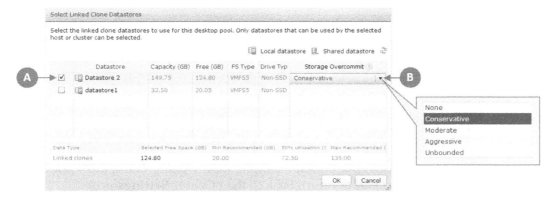

This configuration box allows you to select the datastore that is going to be used for the linked-clone virtual desktop machines to be stored. In this example, we are going to tick **Datastore 2 (A)** as our datastore. Ideally, this datastore would be fast storage of some description.

The **Storage Overcommit** (**B**) feature allows you to place more linked-clone virtual desktop machines onto a datastore than you can by using full clones. With linked clones, you can have a logical storage space that is bigger than the actual capacity of that datastore, hence the name overcommit. The overcommit option allows you to configure a set number of virtual desktop machines per datastore with the following settings to determine that number of linked clones:

- **None**: This indicates no overcommitment.
- **Conservative**: This allows four times the size of the datastore.
- **Moderate**: This allows seven times the size of the datastore.
- **Aggressive**: This allows 15 times the size of the datastore.
- **Unbounded**: This leaves no limit to the number of linked clones on the datastore. When using this option, ensure that there is enough storage capacity, both for now and for future growth.

For example, if you have a 100 GB datastore and each linked clone was 20 GB, then without storage overcommit you could have five virtual desktop machines on this datastore. If you now set the storage overcommit to moderate, you can now accommodate 35 linked-clone virtual desktop machines on that datastore.

Click on **OK** to return back to the **vCenter Settings** page.

Click on **Browse** (**31**) next to **Replica disk datastores**. You will see the following screenshot:

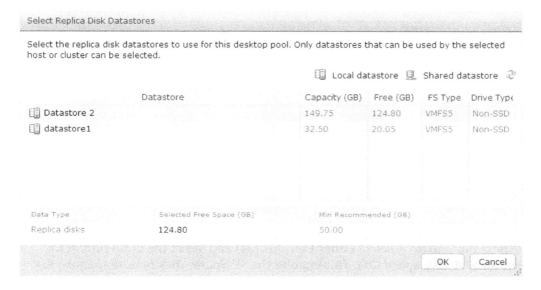

We are again going to choose **Datastore 2** for our replica disk to be stored on, so click on **Datastore 2**. Ideally, we would want to use an SSD-based datastore.

Click on **OK** to return back to the **vCenter Settings** page.

We have now completed all the vCenter configuration settings. Check the configuration page to make sure everything is configured correctly and then click on **Next** to move to the **Advanced Storage Options** configuration page.

On this configuration page, you can configure some of the advanced features of vSphere storage management. Check the box for **Use View Storage Accelerator** (**32**). This enables the content-based read cache feature on the ESX host, which caches the most commonly read blocks into memory. You can have up to 2 GB configured as a cache. You can then decide the **Disk Types** (**33**) to which the accelerator will apply to. In our example, we will select **OS disks**. All this is shown in the following screenshot:

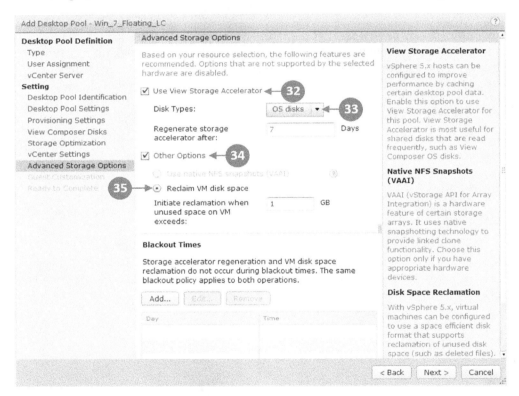

The next thing to do is select **Other Options** (**34**) and select the radio button for **Reclaim VM disk space** (**35**). This enables the SE Sparse disk feature to make the most efficient use of the available disk space.

The final option you can set here is **Blackout Times**. This sets time periods whereby the ESXi hosts will not perform any operations on the virtual desktop machines, allowing them to concentrate on key tasks. This is especially important during user log-on time or when you know the virtual desktop workload is high.

Click on **Next** to move to the **Guest Customization** configuration page. On this final configuration page, we are going to tell vCenter how we want our newly built virtual desktop machine to be customized.

First, select the domain that this virtual desktop machine is going to be part of. Click on the drop-down menu and select **pvolab.com(administrator) (36)**.

Next, we need to select the **AD Container** that this virtual desktop machine will live in. Click on **Browse (37)** and then select the container you want to use. In our example, we will use the **Horizon View Desktops** folder, so click on **OU=Horizon View Desktops (38)**. This is shown in the following screenshot:

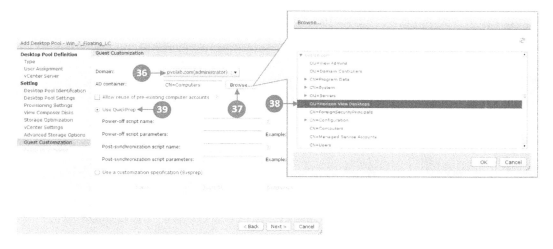

One of the key parts of the customization process is preparing the actual virtual desktop machine. There are two options we can use in Horizon View: the VMware QuickPrep tool or Microsoft Sysprep. In our example, we are going to use QuicPrep, so click on the radio button for **Use QuickPrep (39)**.

There are a few key differences between the two, which are detailed in the following screenshot:

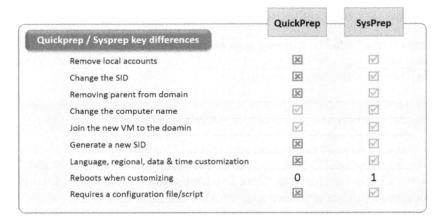

Quickprep / Sysprep key differences	QuickPrep	SysPrep
Remove local accounts	☒	☑
Change the SID	☒	☑
Removing parent from domain	☒	☑
Change the computer name	☑	☑
Join the new VM to the doamin	☑	☑
Generate a new SID	☒	☑
Language, regional, data & time customization	☒	☑
Reboots when customizing	0	1
Requires a configuration file/script	☒	☑

So what does QuickPrep do? As each new virtual desktop machine starts for the first time, QuickPrep will create a new computer account in AD for each new machine that gets created. It then gives each linked clone a new name based on the naming pattern that you chose and then joins that machine to your domain.

Click on **Next** to move to the **Ready to Complete** page. We have now completed the desktop pool configuration. Review the settings you have entered and when happy with these, click on **Finish**.

At the top-right hand side of the page, you will see a tick box for **Entitle Users** after finishing this wizard. If you tick this, you will automatically go to the user entitlement page. We will do this manually in the next section, but before we do this, let's quickly go and check whether our newly created virtual desktop machines have been created.

Switch to the **vSphere Web Client** and navigate to the **hzn6-vcs1.pvolab.com** vCenter Server (**39**), as shown in the following screenshot:

You can see that the replica folder has been created (**40**). If you then look in the **Win_7_Floating_LC** folder that we created, you will see the two virtual desktop machines (**41**), **Win7-vm1**, and **Win7-vm2**, as per our chosen naming convention.

Entitling users to a desktop pool

Now that we have created our pool, we need to entitle end users to it so that they can start consuming the virtual desktop machines in the pool.

1. From the View Administrator console, click on **Desktop Pools** (**1**) from the **Inventory** section. Then, click **Entitlements** (**2**) and select **Add entitlement...** (**3**). This is shown in the following screenshot:

2. You will now see the **Add Entitlements** dialog box. To add a user, click on **Add...** (**4**). You will then see the **Find User or Group** dialog box, as shown in the following screenshot:

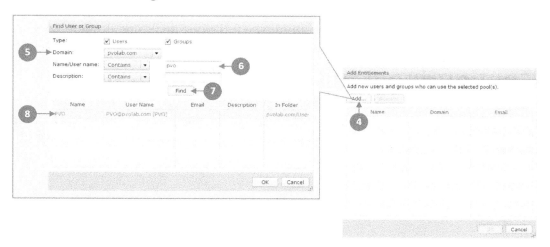

3. Click on the drop-down menu for **Domain** (**5**) and ensure it reflects the domain in which the user you want to entitle resides; in our case, it's **pvolab.com**.

4. We can then search by **Name/User Name**; so in the box (**6**), type the name of the user you want to entitle. In our example, the username is **pvo**. Then, click on **Find** (**7**).

5. You will now see the details of the user appear in the box (**8**). Select the username and then click on **OK**.

If we now switch back to View Administrator, we can see the details of our desktop pool and the fact that it has one user that has been entitled (**9**) and that the pool has been enabled (**10**), as shown in the following screenshot:

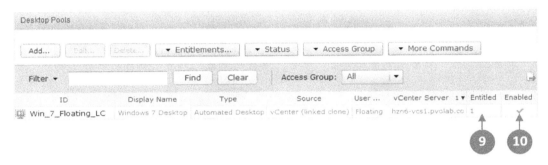

We have now successfully created a desktop pool containing our virtual desktop machines, with a floating assignment and provisioned as linked clones. In the next section, we will cover the process for building a full-clone dedicated desktop pool.

Configuring a full-clone desktop pool

The process in which you build a full-clone dedicated desktop pool is not too similar to the linked clone floating process we described in the previous section. In this section, we will briefly cover how to build a dedicated, full-clone desktop pool. Have a look at the following screenshot:

1. From the **Inventory** section, click on **Desktop Pools (1)** and then click on **Add... (2)**.

2. Click on the radio button for **Automated Desktop Pool** from the pool type menu. Click on **Next** to continue.

3. On the **User Assignment** page, click on the radio button for **Dedicated** and tick the box for **Enable automatic assignment**. Click on **Next** to continue.

4. Click on the radio button for **Full virtual machines** on the vCenter Server configuration page. This means that the virtual desktop machines will be built from the gold image template that we built previously. Click on **Next** to continue.

5. Enter the details for the **Desktop Pool Identification** on the next configuration page. In this example, we will give the pool the **ID** of Win_8_Dedicated and enter the display name Windows 8.1 Desktop. Click on **Next** to continue.

6. On the **Desktop Pool Settings** configuration page, set the details as per the configuration we used for the previous pool. Click on **Next** to continue.

7. Next, we need to configure the **Provisioning Settings**. Ensure that you check the boxes for **Enable provisioning** and **Stop provisioning on error**. You then need to enter a naming pattern. In our example, we use the naming convention **Win8-vm{1}** and we will click on the radio button for **Provision all machines up-front**. Click on **Next** to continue.

8. Click on **Next** on the **Storage Optimization** page.

9. On the **vCenter Settings** page, enter the following details:

   ° **Template**: Navigate to the Windows 8 Gold Image template.

   ° **Virtual Machine Location**: Select the **View Desktops** folder.

   ° **Host or cluster**: In our example, we are going to use the **hzn6-esx1.pvolab.com** host server.

   ° **Resource pool**: Select the resource pool to use for these virtual desktop machines. In our example, we will use **hzn6-esx1.pvolab.com** as our host server because we don't have a resource pool configured.

   ° **Datastores**: Tick the box for **Datastore 2**.

10. Click on **Next** to continue.

11. On **Advanced Storage Options**, tick the box for **Use View Storage Accelerator** and click on **Next** to continue.

12. Next, choose a **Guest Customization** option. In our example, click on the radio button for **None**. If you already have a customization script, you can click on **Use this customization specification**.

13. Finally, you will see the **Ready to Complete** page. Check the settings and click on **Finish** when you are happy to continue.

You will now see that the Windows 8 virtual desktop machine has been built and is named **Win8-vm1** as per our naming pattern that we configured (**4**) and placed into the correct folder, **Win_8_Dedicated** (**3**):

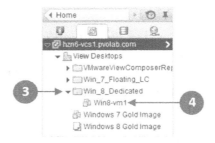

With the Windows 8 dedicated pool now configured, the final step of the process is now to entitle users to use it, as described in the previous section.

Creating a desktop pool for high-end graphics

In the previous sections, we covered creating desktop pools for two different operating system environments with a desktop pool for each.

Another use case of creating a desktop pool is when you have a specific hardware configuration, namely the use of high-end graphics cards for either vSGA or vDGA. In the previous chapter, we also built a GPU-enabled virtual desktop machine, and in this section, we will build a desktop pool for this virtual desktop machine.

To create the desktop pool, perform the following steps:

1. From the **Inventory** section, click on **Desktop Pools** (**1**) and then click on **Add...** (**2**) (as shown in an earlier screenshot).

2. Click on the radio button for **Manual Desktop Pool** from the pool type menu. Click on **Next** to continue.

3. On the **User Assignment** page, click on the radio button for **Dedicated** and make sure that the box for **Enable automatic assignment** is not selected. Click on **Next** to continue.

4. Click on the radio button for **vCenter virtual machines** on the **Machine Source** configuration page. This means that the virtual desktop machines will be listed from the vCenter Server. Click on **Next** to continue.

5. On the **vCenter Server** page, select the vCenter Server that manages the hosts and virtual desktop machines you want to use.

6. Enter the details for the **Desktop Pool Identification** on the next configuration page. In this example, we will give the pool the **ID** of vDGA_Desktops and enter the display name Windows 7 vDGA. Click on **Next** to continue.

7. You will now see the **Desktop Pool Settings** configuration page, as shown in the following screenshot. Most of the settings are the same as we set for the previous pools, but we need to change some settings in the **Remote Display Protocol** section.

   Ensure that the **Default display protocol** is set to **PCoIP (1)**. To allow View to make use of the advanced graphics settings, you need to make sure that you set the **Allow users to choose protocol** option is set to **No (2)**; the reason is that these features only work with PCoIP. If you leave the option set to **Yes**, then the **3D Renderer** section will remain grayed out and you won't be able to select the option for **Automatic (3)**, as shown in the following screenshot:

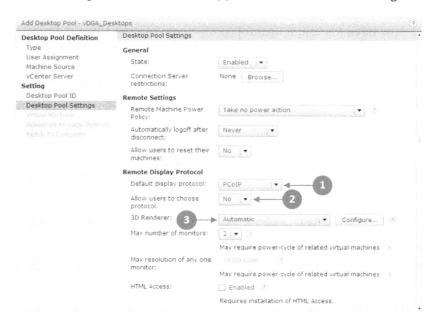

There are four different options for the 3D Renderer:

- ○ **Automatic**: ESX reserves GPU resources on a first-come-first-served basis and if they can't be fulfilled, it will revert to software rendering
- ○ **Software**: ESX uses software rendering only
- ○ **Hardware**: Like the **Automatic option**, ESX reserves GPU resources on a first-come-first-served basis and if they can't be fulfilled, the virtual desktop machine will not power on
- ○ **Disabled**: This option would leave no 3D rendering configured

The other option you have is to configure the amount of video memory allocated to that virtual desktop machine. Click on **Configure...** next to the **3D Renderer** option. You can adjust the slider bar to configure 64 MB up to 512 MB of VRAM.

8. On the **Virtual Machine** settings configuration page under **Add vCenter Virtual Machines,** search for the virtual desktop machines you may want to add to this desktop pool. You can either tick the box to show all virtual machines or use the **Filter** option to search for specific machines. Select each of the machines you want to add to the pool and then click on **Add**.

9. On the **Advanced Storage Options**, check the box to **Use View Storage Accelerator** and click on **Next** to continue.

10. Finally, you will see the **Ready to Complete** page. Check the settings and click on **Finish** when you are happy to continue.

You should now have a manual desktop pool created in the View Administrator that contains your dedicated GPU-enabled virtual desktop machines. There is one final thing you need to configure, but you can do that only by connecting to the virtual desktops using View.

Once you have connected to the virtual desktop machine, open a command prompt window and navigate to the directory C:\program files\common files\VMware\ Teradici PCOIP Server\.

From that directory, run the following command:

```
Montereyenable.exe - enable
```

This enables the NVIDIA APIs. Reboot the virtual desktop machine when complete.

You should now have a working GPU-enabled virtual desktop machine that you can start to entitle to users. To do this, follow the steps that we described in the *Entitling users to a desktop pool* section of this chapter.

If you want to make sure that the virtual desktop machine is using the vDGA and the NVIDIA graphics card, click on the **Start** button and then click on **Run**. In the **Run** dialog box, type the command dxdiag and click on **OK**. The **DirectX Diagnostic Tool** will launch. Click on the **Display** tab at the top. You will see the following screenshot:

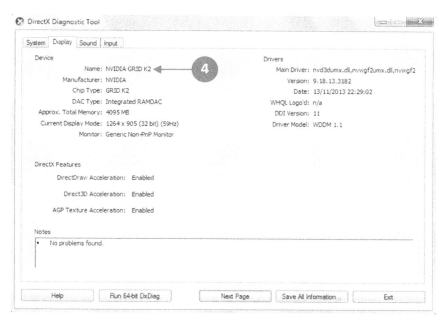

You can see that the graphics card in use is **NVIDIA GRID K2** (**4**).

> One thing to note is that vDGA will not work when opening a console session in the virtual desktop machine from the vSphere Web Client. You won't see anything displayed in the console.

Summary

In this chapter, we configured the Horizon View Administrator to deliver our virtual desktop machines. We built and configured three different desktop pools—a linked-clone Windows 7 pool with a floating assignment, a dedicated, full-clone Windows 8 pool, and finally a dedicated Windows 7 pool with GPU hardware-enabled virtual desktop machines.

In the next chapter, we will look at the client options for connecting to the virtual desktop machines within the desktop pools that we have just configured.

8
Horizon View Clients

Let's quickly take stock of where we have gotten to with deploying our Horizon View environment. So far, we have looked at the architecture and design, performed an installation, built our virtual desktop machines, and configured the View Administrator to prepare the virtual desktop machine for delivery to the end users. However, the question is, "how are we going to connect our endpoint devices to our virtual desktop machine?" This is where the Horizon View Client comes in.

In this chapter, we are going to look at the different options available to an end user in order to allow them to connect to their virtual desktop machines, some of the advantages and disadvantages over the different options, and why it matters which one you choose.

This is especially true when it comes to hardware-based clients, and all too often, we see people choose the wrong client device for their use case. It's not a case of buying the cheapest, smallest device; it's about choosing the device that does the job the user requires of it.

The Horizon View software client

The Horizon View Client is a software application that gets installed onto the end user's device, which allows them to log in and connect to their virtual desktop machine. Once logged in, the View Client displays the screen from the virtual desktop machine located in the data center onto the screen of the local client device.

The client software is available for the following platforms:

- Microsoft Windows
- Apple Mac
- iOS

- Android
- Linux

Downloading the Horizon View Clients

The Horizon View Clients are available on the VMware download page at `http://tinyurl.com/q2o98kh`.

In our example, we are going to download the View Client software and save it in the shared folder.

 One thing to note is that the Horizon View Client software has a different release cycle from the main Horizon View software, which means that the clients are released on a more frequent basis and you don't have to wait for a full Horizon View release to take advantage of new client-based features. You can also use older versions of the View Client, although you might not be able to take advantage of some of the latest features and functionality.

Horizon View Client for Windows platforms

In this section, we are going to install the Horizon View Client for Windows on our control desktop and look at how to configure it:

1. Navigate to the location of the installation software. In our example, this is in the `\\hzn6-dc\Shared Folder\View 6.0\View Clients` shared folder. There is one version for 32-bit operating systems and one for 64-bit operating systems.

2. Launch the `VMware-Horizon-View-Client-x86-3.0.0-1887158` installation program for the View Client.

3. On the **Welcome to the VMware Horizon View Client Setup Wizard** page, click on **Next**.

4. Tick the **I accept the terms in the License Agreement** box, and then click on **Next**.

5. You will now see the **Custom Setup** box. You will see a couple of options that you can choose from: the first option is to install the components in order to allow the USB redirection from the endpoint to the virtual desktop machine and the second is to allow you to log in to the virtual desktop machine as the current user, who is logged into that endpoint device already.

This is shown in the following screenshot:

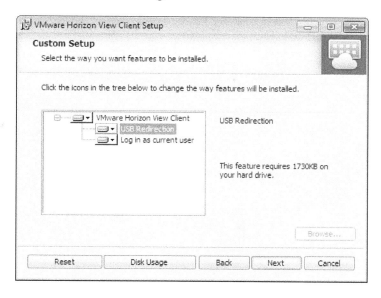

6. Click on **Next**.

7. In the **Default Server** dialog box, enter the address of the default connection server that the users will first connect to (**1**). In our example, the address of the connection server is **hzn6-cs1.pvolab.com**, which we will enter as shown in the following screenshot. You can leave this field blank and add it later.

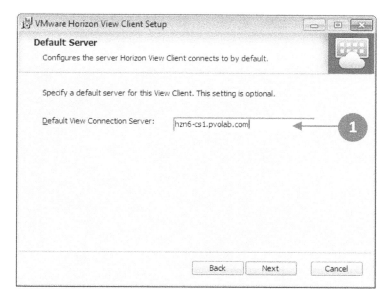

8. Click on **Next**.

In the **Enhanced Single Sign On** dialog box, you can decide how the **Login as current user** feature behaves. You can allow the option to be shown in the options menu (**2**) to the end user or set it to log in as the current user by default (**3**), which means that the user will not need to log in again when connecting to their virtual desktop machine.

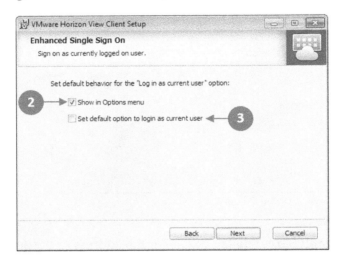

9. Click on **Next**.

10. In the **Configure Shortcuts** dialog box, choose whether or not you want a shortcut on the desktop of the endpoint device (**4**) or for it to show on the **Start** menu (**5**).

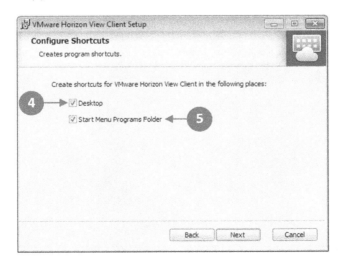

11. Click on **Next**.

12. In the **Ready to install VMware Horizon View Client** dialog box, click on **Install** to start the installation process and copy the necessary files and configuration details.

13. The installation will then get completed. In the **Completed the VMware Horizon View Client Setup Wizard** dialog box, click on **Finish** to complete the installation.

14. You will then be prompted to reboot the endpoint device. Click on **Yes** to reboot.

15. When the device reboots, you will see that a new program has been installed, which is the **VMware Horizon View Client**, as shown in the following screenshot (**6**):

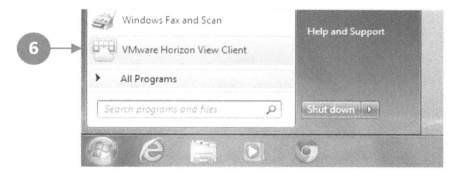

With the client installed, we will look at the configuration options in the next section.

Launching and configuring the Horizon View Client

Launch the Horizon View Client application. You will now see the following screenshot:

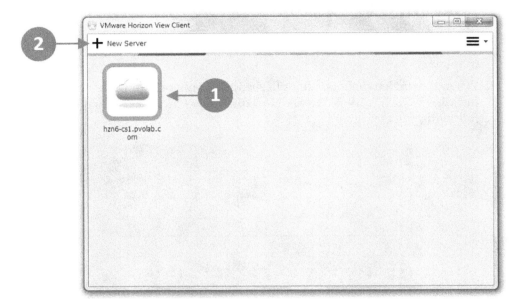

The steps to be performed in order to launch and configure the Horizon View Client are as follows:

1. You will see that our default connection server is shown as an icon (**1**) in the dialog box.

2. If you want to add an additional connection server, click on the **+ New Server** button in the top-left corner (**2**). You will then be prompted for the address of the new connection server.

3. You also have some other configuration options available by clicking on the down arrow in the top-right corner of the client application (**3**).

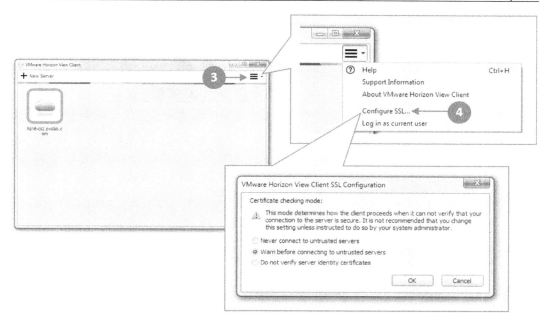

4. The key option is the **Configure SSL...** option **(4)**, which configures the certificate-checking mode and allows you to potentially connect without verifying the certificate.

The other useful option is **Support Information**, which allows you to collect support information in order to help with diagnosing client issues.

Testing the connection to the desktop

In this section, we will test whether we can connect to our virtual desktop machines using the Horizon View Client and the desktop pools we set up in *Chapter 7, Configuring Horizon View to Deliver Virtual Desktops*.

From the control desktop machine that we just installed the Horizon View Client on, ensure that the View Client is running.

Perform the following steps to test the connection to the desktop:

1. Double-click on the box with the name of our connection server; in our example, this is `hzn6-cs1.pvolab.com`. Enter the username and password for the user that we want to log in as. We will use the username `pvo`.

2. Click on **Login**. This is shown in the following screenshot:

3. Once logged in, you will see the following dialog box. This dialog box shows you the desktop pools to which our user has been entitled. In our example, this particular user is entitled to the **Windows 7 Desktop** pool and the **Windows 8.1 Desktop** pool.

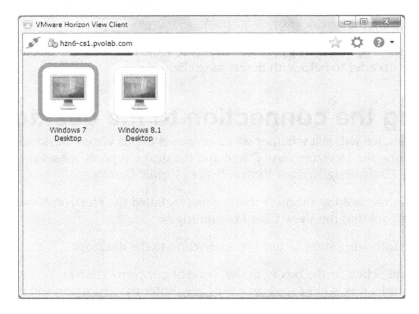

If you double-click on one of the desktop pool icons, you will be connected to a desktop from within that pool.

Horizon View Client for Mac

The Horizon View Client is also available for Apple Mac, and it looks and feels the same as the Windows desktop version, as shown in the following screenshot:

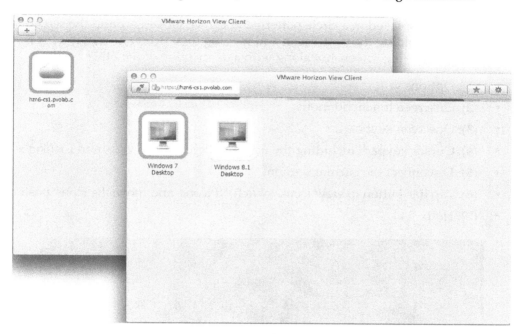

Horizon View Client for iPad

As with the Mac client, the iPad client has a familiar View Client look and feel, as shown in the following screenshot:

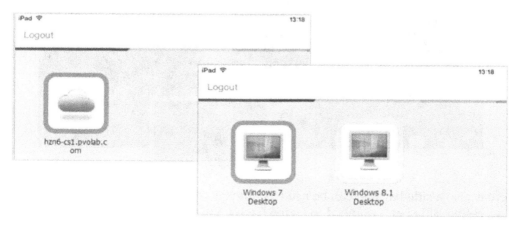

In addition to the standard client, the iPad and Android versions have the **Unity Touch** feature that allows you to better interact with the Windows virtual desktop machines. Unity Touch gives you the ability to access features such as onscreen keyboard and onscreen touchpad mouse.

These icons are displayed in a circle pattern and can be moved around the screen by pressing and holding the center icon and moving to where you want it. This is shown in the following screenshot along with a description of the other buttons:

- (1): Options
- (2): Onscreen touchpad mouse
- (3): Onscreen keyboard
- (4): Cursor keypad, including the *Page Up*, *Page Down*, *Home*, and *Ctrl* keys
- (5): Disconnect the current session
- (6): Tap this button to view icons, switch off icons, and move the icons' position
- (7): Help

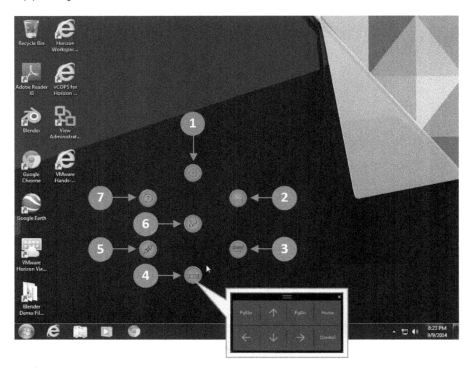

There is also a side bar that can be used as quick access to your applications. To access the side bar, you need to swipe from left to right on the screen.

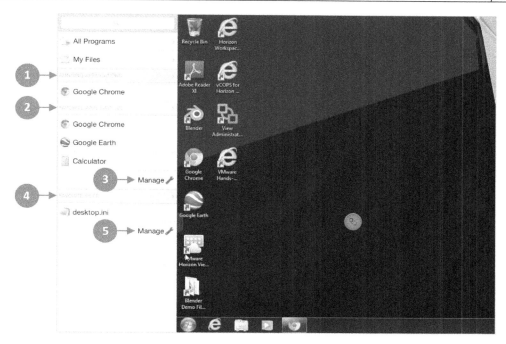

The side bar is customizable and you are able to change your favorite applications and files, as shown in the previous screenshot:

1. View your current running application (**1**).
2. View your current favorite application (**2**).
3. Click on **Manage** (**3**) to add and remove applications to your favorites.
4. View your current favorite files (**4**).
5. Click on **Manage** (**5**) to add and remove files to your favorites.

Browser-based desktop access

There are some use cases where installing the client software on the endpoint device is not possible, for example, somebody using a Chromebook or a public-facing endpoint in a hotel lobby where you do not have the ability to install software. In this case, you can access your virtual desktop machine using an HTML5-enabled web browser. The HTML access to the desktop is referred to as **VMware Blast**.

Although perfectly usable, browser access is not as performant as using a client-based device, and you don't get the full feature-rich experience you might need.

To connect to your virtual desktop machine using a browser, open the browser and type in the address of your connection server; in our example lab, this is `https://hzn6-cs1.pvolab.com`.

You will then see an option screen from where you can either download the View Client or connect via HTML, as shown in the following screenshot:

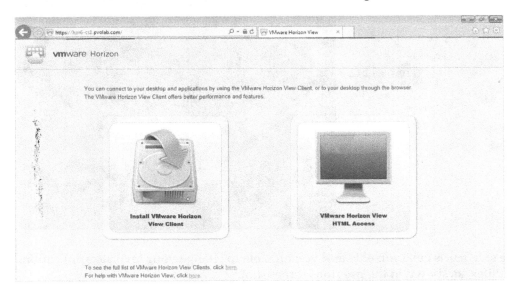

You can configure this screen to not show the client download option if you want to:

1. Click on the **VMware Horizon View HTML Access** button. You will then be prompted to log in.

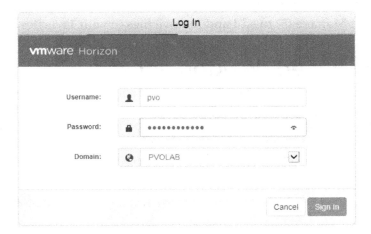

2. Enter the username and password, and then click on **Sign in**.

   In the next screen, you will see that you are given the option of choosing the desktop from the pool that you are entitled to. In our example, the user is entitled to just the Windows 8 desktop pool, and not the Windows 7 pool that we can access using the Windows and Mac client.

3. Click on the **Windows 8.1 Desktop** icon. Your virtual desktop machine will then open in a tab on your browser, as shown in the following screenshot:

In the next section, we are going to cover the hardware-based client options.

Hardware-based clients and thin clients

When it comes to hardware-based clients, there are a few options which, other than the hardware specification, vary by the operating system that they run. We will start with zero clients.

Zero clients

Zero clients are so called, because they have no operating system and use the Teradici PCoIP chipset instead. This means that they require very little maintenance and will typically perform better than using a software-based client or even an endpoint device with local CPU and GPU resources, as they use dedicated hardware designed purely to decode PCoIP.

The one thing to be aware of is that if you require an endpoint device that requires a local OS to run something like client-side rendering or a unified communication solution that requires particular codecs to be installed, zero clients will not be the right device.

Thin clients

Thin clients differ from zero clients in that they do have a local operating system installed on them. This local OS is typically either Windows- or Linux-based, running some form of connection client software; however, it is important to check whether they support the features that the user requires.

The advantages of using thin clients are down to the cost of the device and lower power consumption. You can also potentially run more features, especially if you choose a Windows-based device. However, this is a disadvantage as well, given the fact that you will need to manage the OS on the thin-client devices.

Summary

In this chapter, we have taken a closer look at the options for connecting from our endpoint device to the virtual desktop machine.

We also installed the Horizon View Client for Windows and configured it and made it ready for use as well as discussed some of the other options around hardware-based clients.

In the next chapter, we will use the client to connect to the virtual desktop machine in our example lab, and then look at the options for fine-tuning the end user experience.

9

Fine-tuning the End User Experience

We have now almost completed our Horizon View deployment and delivered virtual desktop machines to the end users; however, in this chapter, we are going to look at how we can fine-tune the end user experience. In the same way as we optimized the operating system to run as a virtual desktop machine, we need to ensure that we are delivering the best experience and performance across the network to our end users.

The first thing we will look at is putting in place the policies that help control the end user experience, along with what users are able to do, from within their virtual desktop machine, all of which is controlled and managed from Active Directory.

In order to deliver this policy-based delivery, we need to prepare Active Directory with some Horizon-View-specific administrative templates and configuration.

We will then go on to look at how we can measure and optimize the delivery protocol, which is PCoIP.

Active Directory prerequisites

The behavior of a virtual desktop machine is governed by an Active Directory policy. The policy configures things such as graphics experience and cut and paste options, to name a few.

To make life easier, the templates for these policies have already been created and can be found in **Horizon View GPO Bundle**, which we downloaded and saved to the shared folder in *Chapter 4, Installing Horizon View 6.0.*

If you unzip this file, you will see that it contains 12 **Administrative Templates** (**ADM**). We will add these in the *Importing and applying the Horizon View ADM templates* section of this chapter.

In the next sections, we will cover how to install these templates and create the Active Directory requirements for Horizon View.

Creating an organizational unit

First, we need to create a new **Organizational Unit (OU)** for our virtual desktop machines. It's a best practice to have a separate OU for virtual desktop machines to ensure that we don't apply the wrong policies to them, which can potentially impact the performance, and vice versa. We don't want to apply VDI-based policies to our physical estate, and also you should also block any inheritance of existing policies to the virtual desktop machines.

Create a new OU in Active Directory; in our example lab, we have called this **Horizon View Desktops**.

Depending on your own environment, you might want to create an OU for different use cases or maybe different departments within your organization. This would allow you to apply different View-based policies to each OU, which could be based on that particular use case, maybe a policy specific for LAN users.

Next, as we have already created some virtual desktop machines, we will move them into the newly created OU. In the following sections, we'll move the Windows 7 gold image machine.

Click on **Computers**, highlight **WIN7-VM**, and then right-click on it. Click on **Move...**, and then select the location to move to. In our example, we will move to the **Horizon View Desktops** OU. Click on **OK** to complete the task.

Next, we will create a GPO to link to this OU.

Creating Group Policy Objects for Horizon View

Now that we have an OU created for our virtual desktop machines, we can create **Group Policy Objects (GPO)** to link to the OU; in our example lab, we'll call this policy **View Desktop Policy**:

1. From the **Start** menu, select **Run...**, and type MMC to open the management console. Next, you need to add the snap-in for **Group Policy Management**.

2. You will now have the Group Policy Management console displayed. Expand the **Forest: pvolab.com**, **Domains**, and **pvolab.com** entries, and then highlight the **Horizon View Desktops** OU (**1**) that we created previously.

3. Right-click and then select **Create a GPO in this domain, and Link it here...** (**2**). Type in the name for the new policy. As we mentioned previously, we will call this policy View Desktop Policy (**3**).

   This is shown in the following screenshot:

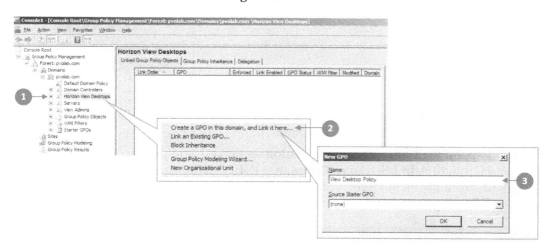

4. Click on **OK** when you have finished.

Importing and applying the Horizon View ADM templates

With our OU created and a group policy linked to it, we can now import the specific ADM templates to the GPO and start to configure the behavior of the policy. In our example, we will import all the templates into this GPO; however, as we previously discussed, you might want to divide up different templates and GPO settings into different OUs, depending on your own individual environment:

1. Highlight the newly created GPO (1), and then right-click on it.

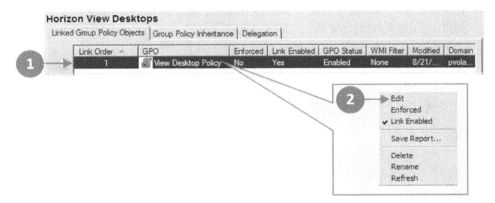

2. From the menu, click on **Edit** (2) to edit the policy. The **Group Policy Management Editor** will now launch.

3. Expand the **Computer Configuration** section (3), and then expand **Policies**. Highlight **Administrative Templates: Policy definitions** (4) and right-click on it. From the menu, select **Add/Remove Templates...** (5). This is shown in the following screenshot:

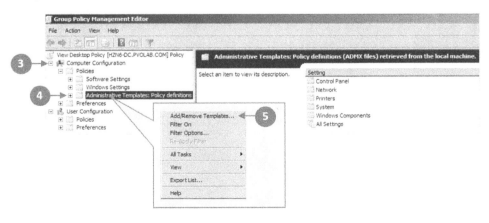

4. You will now see the **Add/Remove Templates** dialog box.

5. Click on **Add…** (6) to add the Horizon View ADM templates. You will then see the dialog box from where you can select the location of where the templates are stored:

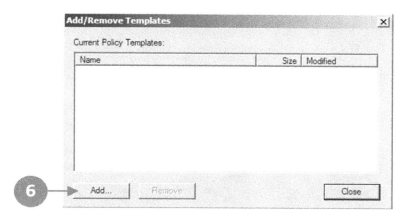

6. In our example lab, the templates are located in the shared folder. Once located, highlight all the files in the folder (7) and click on **Open**, as shown in the previous screenshot. You will now see that the templates have been added (8). Click on **Close**:

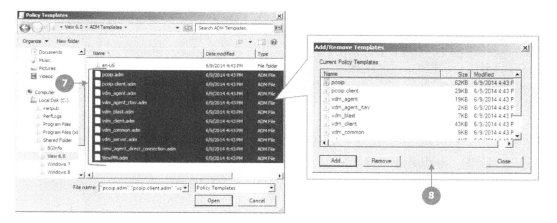

7. You will also see that the templates are now visible under the **Classic Administrative Templates (ADM)** section (**9**) from where you can now start to configure the policies.

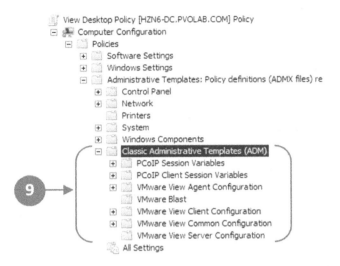

We will look at one of the policies in more detail later in this chapter.

Enabling the loopback policy

In a VDI model and particularly with floating desktop assignments, we have multiple users accessing the same desktop. To ensure that any configuration changes that a user makes to one of the virtual desktop machines apply to all of the users who use that machine, we need to enable the loopback processing feature. This is described in the following steps:

1. From the **Group Policy Management Editor** screen in the **Computer Configuration** section, expand **Policies (1)**, **Administrative Templates: Policy definitions (ADM) (2)**, and then **System (3)**.

2. Highlight **Group Policy (4)**. You will then see the policy options listed in the right-hand side window.

3. Scroll down to **User Group Policy loopback processing mode (5)** and click to select it. This is shown in the following screenshot:

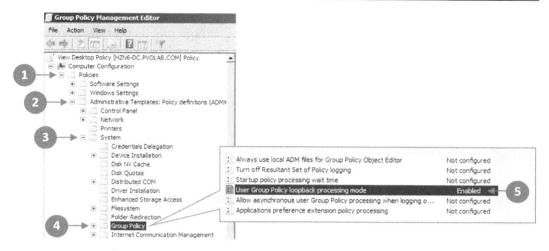

4. From the menu that appears, click on **Edit** to change the setting. The following dialog box appears:

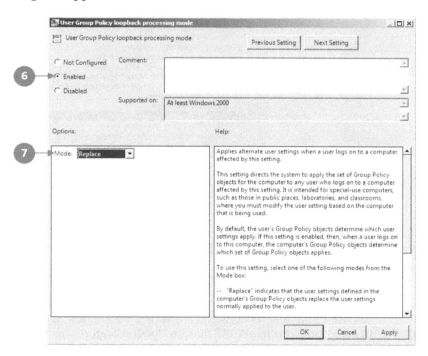

5. Enable the loopback setting by clicking on the radio button for **Enabled** (6). You can then choose the mode that the loopback operates in, which is either **Replace** or **Merge** (7).

With the **Replace** option, the user policy applied is just what is associated with the computer. Any user policies are ignored. Choosing **Merge** means that the policies applied are both the user- and computer-related policies, where the computer policy wins in the event of a conflict.

Example policy settings

In this section, we are going to examine one of the policies in more detail, and for this example, we have deliberately chosen the PCoIP image quality setting, as this setting is set quite high by default:

1. From the **Group Policy Management Editor** screen, navigate to **Classic Administrative Templates (ADM) | PCoIP Session Variables**, and then go to **Overridable Administrator Defaults (1)**:

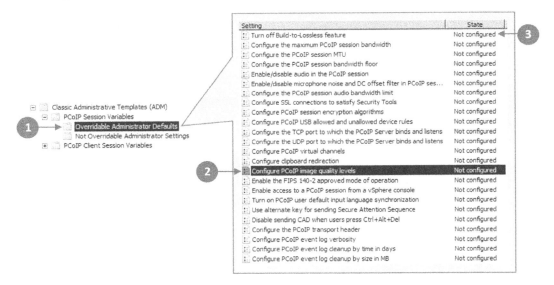

2. Select **Configure PCoIP image quality levels (2)**, right-click on it, and select **Edit**.

> One thing that needs to be quickly highlighted for anyone who has used previous versions of View is that before View 6, the default option for the PCoIP build-to-lossless feature was that it was enabled, which means that you required more bandwidth for that level of image detail. In View 6, the default is for build-to-lossless to be disabled (**3**).

3. You will now see the configuration dialog box shown in the following screenshot. The first thing to do is set the policy to **Enabled** (**4**).

4. Once enabled, you have the option to set the minimum (**5**) and maximum (**6**) image quality settings.

However, the key setting here is the **Frame Rate** setting (**7**). By default, this is set to 30 frames per second whether you have this policy set to **Disabled** or **Not Configured**, which means that this is the value that gets applied. This is fine if you have loads of bandwidth and users who require video playback; however, for standard users, you would want to throttle this back to somewhere between 12 to 15 frames per second.

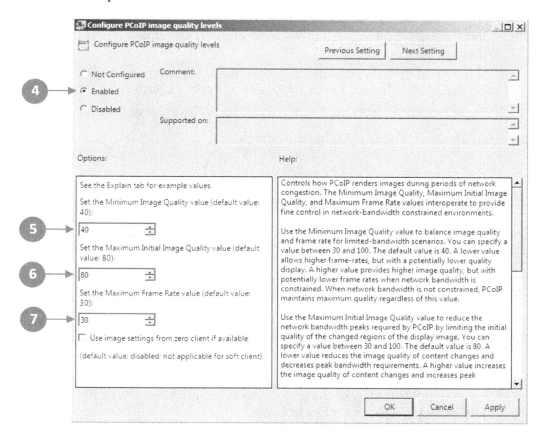

The PCoIP tuning tool

The final thing to cover in this chapter is dynamically tuning the virtual desktop machines using the PCoIP tuning tool, which is available on the web page link at http://tinyurl.com/ocqxykn.

Once you have the tool downloaded, launch the tool on the virtual desktop machine that you want to tune. You will see that you have a number of options to choose from:

- **Activate Profile (1)**: This allows you to activate a preset profile based on a default user, WAN user, and a task worker.

- **Manage Profiles (2)**: This allows you to adjust the settings of a particular profile. You can dynamically change the image quality, frames per second, and bandwidth and switch on build-to-lossless. To activate a profile, you will need to reboot.

- **Show Session Stats (3)**: This shows you the actual usage for things such as the bandwidth, frames per second, latency, and CPU utilization.

- **Show Session Health (4)**: This shows you a health score of the PCoIP session.

These options are shown in the following screenshot:

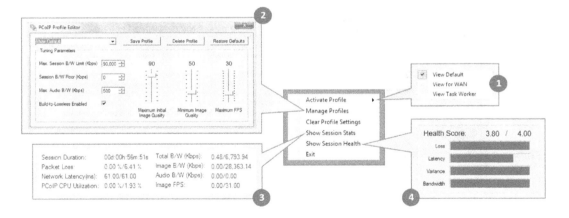

For a more in-depth overview of the performance and potential issues, it's worth installing vCenter Operations for Horizon View.

Summary

In this chapter, we looked at how to start fine-tuning the performance and experience for the end user session with their virtual desktop machine.

We covered how to prepare Active Directory with Horizon-View-specific policies and administrative templates in order to define how the virtual desktop machine behaves and also the experience for the end user. As you can see, there are a number of options you can configure within the templates, and we just highlighted one specific setting as an example, as it is also a key setting that will need to be changed.

Finally, we looked at one of the many tools available in order to help in the tuning process.

We have now successfully built and configured our entire Horizon View environment, from the infrastructure components to building and optimizing desktop images.

References

In this appendix, you will find some additional information and useful links.

The VMware official documentation

The following are some useful links:

- **Horizon View architecture planning document**:
  http://tinyurl.com/omyyhpg

- **View installation**: http://tinyurl.com/n6zybno

- **View Admin guide**: http://tinyurl.com/p7pfctp

- **Cloud Pod Architecture admin**: http://tinyurl.com/p2uso3q

- **View security**: http://tinyurl.com/nehwya9

- **Migrating user profiles**: http://tinyurl.com/lmgjr4t

- **View documentation center**: http://tinyurl.com/lqrrmlq

- **VMware ThinApp home page**:
  https://www.vmware.com/products/thinapp/

- **Graphics Acceleration**: http://tinyurl.com/pxvlual

The software's download pages and tools

The software's download pages and tools can be found on the following links:

- **Download page**: https://my.vmware.com/web/vmware/login

- **Horizon View Client download page**: http://tinyurl.com/q2o98kh

- **VDI Calculator**: http://myvirtualcloud.net/?page_id=1076

Summary

In this appendix, we have listed some useful links to official documentation and also software download pages.

Index

Thank you for buying
VMware Horizon View Essentials

About Packt Publishing

Packt, pronounced 'packed', published its first book "Mastering phpMyAdmin for Effective MySQL Management" in April 2004 and subsequently continued to specialize in publishing highly focused books on specific technologies and solutions.

Our books and publications share the experiences of your fellow IT professionals in adapting and customizing today's systems, applications, and frameworks. Our solution based books give you the knowledge and power to customize the software and technologies you're using to get the job done. Packt books are more specific and less general than the IT books you have seen in the past. Our unique business model allows us to bring you more focused information, giving you more of what you need to know, and less of what you don't.

Packt is a modern, yet unique publishing company, which focuses on producing quality, cutting-edge books for communities of developers, administrators, and newbies alike. For more information, please visit our website: www.packtpub.com.

About Packt Enterprise

In 2010, Packt launched two new brands, Packt Enterprise and Packt Open Source, in order to continue its focus on specialization. This book is part of the Packt Enterprise brand, home to books published on enterprise software – software created by major vendors, including (but not limited to) IBM, Microsoft and Oracle, often for use in other corporations. Its titles will offer information relevant to a range of users of this software, including administrators, developers, architects, and end users.

Writing for Packt

We welcome all inquiries from people who are interested in authoring. Book proposals should be sent to author@packtpub.com. If your book idea is still at an early stage and you would like to discuss it first before writing a formal book proposal, contact us; one of our commissioning editors will get in touch with you.

We're not just looking for published authors; if you have strong technical skills but no writing experience, our experienced editors can help you develop a writing career, or simply get some additional reward for your expertise.

PUBLISHING

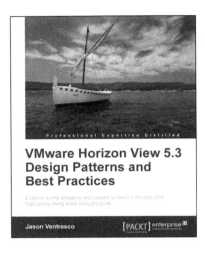

VMware Horizon View 5.3 Design Patterns and Best Practices

ISBN: 978-1-78217-154-6   Paperback: 124 pages

Explore some amazing techniques to build a reliable and high-performing View infrastructure

1. Identify the reasons why you are deploying Horizon View, a critical step to identifying your metrics for success.

2. Determine your Horizon View desktop resource requirements and use them to size your infrastructure.

3. Recognize key design considerations that should influence your Horizon View infrastructure.

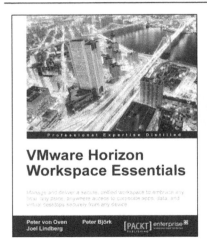

VMware Horizon Workspace Essentials

ISBN: 978-1-78217-237-6   Paperback: 158 pages

Manage and deliver a secure, unified workspace to embrace any time, any place, anywhere access to corporate apps, data, and virtual desktops securely from any device

1. Design, install, and configure a Horizon Workspace infrastructure.

2. Deliver a user's workspace to mobile devices such as Android and iOS.

3. Easy to follow, step-by-step guide on how to deploy and work with Horizon Workspace.

Please check **www.PacktPub.com** for information on our titles

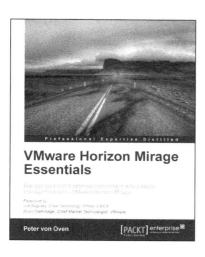

VMware Horizon Mirage Essentials

Peter von Oven

VMware Horizon Mirage Essentials

ISBN: 978-1-78217-235-2   Paperback: 166 pages

Manage your entire desktop environment with a single management tool – VMware Horizon Mirage

1. Deliver a centralized Windows image management solution for physical, virtual, and BYOD.

2. Migrate seamlessly to new versions of operating systems with minimal user downtime.

3. Easy-to-follow, step-by-step guide on how to deploy and work with the technology.

Implementing VMware Horizon View 5.2

Jason Ventresco

Implementing VMware Horizon View 5.2

ISBN: 978-1-84968-796-6   Paperback: 390 pages

A practical guide to designing, implementing, and administrating an optimized Virtual Desktop solution with VMware Horizon View

1. Detailed description of the deployment and administration of the VMware Horizon View suite.

2. Learn how to determine the resources your virtual desktops will require.

3. Design your desktop solution to avoid potential problems and ensure minimal loss of time in the later stages.

Please check **www.PacktPub.com** for information on our titles

www.ingramcontent.com/pod-product-compliance
Lightning Source LLC
Chambersburg PA
CBHW060541060326
40690CB00017B/3562